I0161030

Impetuous Peter

By Ellen G. White

TEACH Services, Inc.
P U B L I S H I N G
www.TEACHServices.com • (800) 367-1844

Copyright © 2017 Ellen G. White

Copyright © 2017 TEACH Services, Inc.

ISBN-13: 978-1-4796-0790-7 (Paperback)

ISBN-13: 978-1-4796-0791-4 (ePub)

ISBN-13: 978-1-4796-0792-1 (Mobi)

Library of Congress Control Number: 2017901690

TEACH Services, Inc.

P U B L I S H I N G

www.TEACHServices.com • (800) 367-1844

Table of Contents

Chapter One

Peter Follows Jesus

Peter Meets Jesus

Andrew sought to impart the joy that filled his heart. Going in search of his brother Simon, he cried, "We have found the Messias." Simon waited for no second bidding. He also had heard the preaching of John the Baptist, and he hastened to the Saviour. The eye of Christ rested upon him, reading his character and his life history. His impulsive nature, his loving, sympathetic heart, his ambition and self-confidence, the history of his fall, his repentance, his labors, and his martyr death,--the Saviour read it all, and He said, "Thou art Simon the son of Jona: thou shalt be called Cephas, which is by interpretation, A stone." *Desire of Ages*, 139.

"Jesus, walking by the Sea of Galilee, saw two brethren, Simon called Peter, and Andrew his brother, casting a net into the sea: for they were fishers. And He saith unto them, Follow Me, and I will make you fishers of men. And they straightway left their nets, and followed Him. And going on from thence, He saw two other brethren, James the son of Zebedee, and John his brother, in a ship with Zebedee their father, mending their nets; and He called them. And they immediately left the ship and their father, and followed Him." [Matthew 4:18-22.]

Christ would make these humble fishermen, in connection with Himself, the means of taking men out of the service of Satan, and placing them in the service of God.

The prompt, unquestioning obedience of these men, with no promise of wages, seems remarkable; but the words of Christ were an invitation that carried with it an impelling power. Christ would make these humble fishermen, in connection with Himself, the means of taking men out of the service of Satan, and placing them in the service of God. In this work they would become his witnesses, bearing to the world His truth unmingled with the traditions and sophistries of men. By practicing His virtues, by walking and working with Him, they were to be qualified to be fishers of men.

Thus were the first disciples appointed to the work of the gospel ministry. For three years they labored in connection with the Saviour, and by His teaching, His works of healing, His example, they were prepared to carry on the work that He began. By the simplicity of faith, by pure, humble service, the disciples were taught to carry responsibilities in God's cause. *Gospel Workers*, 24.

Peter, James, and John sought every opportunity of coming into close contact with their Master, and their desire was granted. Of all the Twelve their relationship to Him was closest. *Education*, 87.

Early Days with Jesus

Day was breaking over the Sea of Galilee. The disciples, weary with a night of fruitless toil, were still in their fishing boats on the lake. Jesus had come to spend a quiet hour by the waterside. In the early morning He hoped for a little season of rest from the multitude that followed Him day after day. But soon the people began to gather about Him. Their numbers rapidly increased, so that He was pressed upon all sides. Meanwhile the disciples had come to land. In order to escape the pressure of the multitude, Jesus stepped into Peter's boat, and bade him pull out a little from the shore. Here Jesus could be better seen and heard by all, and from the boat He taught the multitude on the beach.

The discourse ended, Jesus turned to Peter, and bade him launch out into the sea, and let down his net for a draught. But Peter was disheartened. All night he had taken nothing. During the lonely hours he had thought of the fate of John the Baptist, who was languishing alone in his dungeon. He had thought of the prospect before Jesus and His followers, of the ill success of the mission to Judea, and the malice of the priests and rabbis. Even his own occupation had failed him; and as he watched by the empty nets, the future had seemed dark with discouragement. "Master," he said, "we have toiled all the night, and have taken nothing: nevertheless at Thy word I will let down the net."

Night was the only favorable time for fishing with nets in the clear waters of the lake. After toiling all night without success, it seemed hopeless to cast the net by day; but Jesus had given the command, and love for their Master moved the disciples to obey. Simon and his brother together let down the net. As they attempted to draw it in, so great was the quantity of fish enclosed that it began to break. They were obliged to summon James and John to their aid. When the catch was secured, both the boats were so heavily laden that they were in danger of sinking.

But Peter was unmindful now of boats or lading. This miracle, above any other he had ever witnessed, was to him a manifestation of divine power. In Jesus he saw One who held all nature under His control. The presence of divinity revealed his own unholiness. Love for his Master, shame for his own unbelief, gratitude for the condescension of Christ, above all, the sense of his uncleanness in the presence of infinite purity, overwhelmed him. While his companions were securing the contents of the net, Peter fell at the Saviour's feet, exclaiming, "Depart from me; for I am a sinful man, O Lord." . . .

Peter exclaimed, "Depart from me; for I am a sinful man;" yet he clung to the feet of Jesus, feeling that he could not be parted from Him. The Saviour answered, "Fear not; from henceforth thou shalt catch men." It was after Isaiah had beheld the holiness of God and his own unworthiness that he was entrusted with the divine message. It was after Peter had been led to self-renunciation and dependence upon divine power that he received the call to his work for Christ. *Desire of Ages*, 244-246.

Of the twelve disciples, four were to act a leading part, each in a distinct line. In preparation for this, Christ taught them, foreseeing all. James, destined to swift-coming death by the sword; John, longest of the brethren to follow his Master in labor and persecution; Peter, the pioneer in breaking through the barriers of ages, and teaching the heathen world; and Judas, in service capable of pre-eminence above his brethren, yet brooding in his soul purposes of whose ripening he little dreamed-- these were the objects of Christ's greatest solicitude and the recipients of His most frequent and careful instruction.

Peter, James, and John sought every opportunity of coming into close contact with their Master, and their desire was granted. Of all the Twelve their relationship to Him was closest. *Ministry of Healing*, 86, 87.

Peter's Early Character

Do not seek to exalt self, but learn in the school of Christ meekness and lowliness of heart. You know what Peter's character was, how strikingly his peculiar traits were developed. Before his great fall he was always dictatorial and forward, speaking unadvisedly, from the impulse of the moment. He was always ready to correct others, and to express his mind before he had a clear comprehension of himself or of what he had to say. But Peter was converted, and the converted Peter was very different from the rash, impetuous Peter. He retained his former fervor, but now the grace of Christ regulated his zeal. Instead of being impetuous, self-confident, and self-exalted, he was calm, self-possessed, and teachable. He could then feed the lambs as well as the sheep of Christ's flock. *Testimonies for the Church*, Volume 5, 334.

After his conversion, Peter showed that he was an entirely changed man. He was not the self-confident, boasting Peter that he had been before his conversion. *Review & Herald*, Feb. 26, 1895.

The first pupils of Jesus were chosen from the ranks of the common people. They were humble, unlettered men, these fishers of Galilee; men unschooled in the learning and customs of the rabbis, but trained by the stern discipline of toil and hardship. They were men of native ability and of teachable spirit; men who could be instructed and molded for the Saviour's work. In the common walks of life there is many a toiler patiently treading the round of his daily tasks, unconscious of latent powers that, roused to action, would place him among the world's great leaders. Such were the men who were called by the Saviour to be His colaborers. And they had the advantage of three years' training by the greatest educator this world has ever known. . . .

Bold, aggressive, and self-confident, quick to perceive and forward to act, prompt in retaliation yet generous in forgiving, Peter often erred, and often received reproof.

The history of no one of the disciples better illustrates Christ's method of training than does the history of Peter. Bold, aggressive, and self-confident, quick to perceive and forward to act, prompt in retaliation yet generous in forgiving, Peter often erred, and often received reproof. Nor were his warmhearted loyalty and devotion to Christ the less decidedly recognized and commended. Patiently, with discriminating love, the Saviour dealt with His impetuous disciple, seeking to check his self-confidence, and to teach him humility, obedience, and trust.

But only in part was the lesson learned. Self-assurance was not uprooted.

Often Jesus, the burden heavy upon His own heart, sought to open to the disciples the scenes of His trial and suffering. But their eyes were holden. The knowledge was unwelcome, and they did not see. Self-pity, that shrank from fellowship with Christ in suffering, prompted Peter's remonstrance, "Pity Thyself, Lord: this shall not be unto Thee." Matthew 16:22, margin. His words expressed the thought and feeling of the Twelve.

So they went on, the crisis drawing nearer; they, boastful, con-tentious, in anticipation apportioning regal honors, and dreaming not of the cross.

For them all, Peter's experience had a lesson. To self-trust, trial is defeat. The sure outworking of evil still unforsaken, Christ could not prevent. But as His hand had been outstretched to save when the waves were about to sweep over Peter, so did His love reach out for his rescue when the deep waters swept over his soul. Over and over again, on the very verge of ruin, Peter's words of boasting brought him nearer and still nearer to the brink. Over and over again was given the warning, "Thou shalt . . . deny that thou knowest Me." Luke 22:34. It was the grieved, loving heart of the disciple that spoke out in the avowal, "Lord, I am ready to go with Thee, both into prison, and to death" (Luke 22:33); and He who reads the heart gave to Peter the message, little valued then, but that in the swift-falling darkness would shed a ray of hope: "Simon, Simon, behold, Satan hath desired to have you, that he may sift you as wheat: but I have prayed for thee, that thy faith fail not: and when thou art converted, strengthen thy brethren." Luke 22:31, 32. *Education*, 85-88.

So it was with the disciples previously called. When Jesus bade Peter and his companions follow Him, immediately they left their boats and nets. Some of these disciples had friends dependent on them for support; but when they received the Saviour's invitation, they did not hesitate, and inquire, How shall I live, and sustain my family? They were obedient to the call; and when afterward Jesus asked them, "When I sent you without purse, and scrip, and shoes, lacked ye anything?" they could answer, "Nothing." Luke 22:35.

To Matthew in his wealth, and to Andrew and Peter in their poverty, the same test was brought; the same consecration was made by each. At the moment of success, when the nets were filled with fish, and the impulses of the old life were strongest, Jesus asked the disciples at the sea to leave all for the work of the gospel. So every soul is tested as to whether the desire for temporal good or for fellowship with Christ is strongest. *Desire of Ages*, 273.

The apostles differed widely in habits and disposition. There were the publican, Levi-Matthew, and the fiery zealot Simon, the uncompromising hater of the authority of Rome; the generous, impulsive Peter, and the mean-spirited Judas; Thomas, true-hearted, yet timid and fearful, Philip, slow of heart, and inclined to doubt, and the ambitious, outspoken sons of Zebedee, with their brethren. These were brought together, with their different faults, all with inherited and cultivated tendencies to evil; but in and through Christ they were to dwell in the family of God, learning to become one in faith, in doctrine, in spirit. They would have their tests, their grievances, their differences of opinion; but while Christ was abiding in the heart, there could be no dissension. His love would lead to love for one another; the lessons of the Master would lead to the harmonizing of all differences, bringing the disciples into unity, till they would be of one mind and one judgment. Christ is the great center, and they would approach one another just in proportion as they approached the center. *Desire of Ages*, 296.

There had been a time in Peter's experience when he was unwilling to see the cross in the work of Christ. When the Saviour made known to the disciples His impending sufferings and death, Peter exclaimed, "Be it far from Thee, Lord: this shall not be unto

Thee." Matthew 16:22. Self-pity, which shrank from fellowship with Christ in suffering, prompted Peter's remonstrance. It was to the disciple a bitter lesson, and one which he learned but slowly, that the path of Christ on earth lay through agony and humiliation. But in the heat of the furnace fire he was to learn its lesson. *Acts of the Apostles,* 525.

The stay of Jesus in Samaria was designed to be a blessing to His disciples, who were still under the influence of Jewish bigotry. They felt that loyalty to their own nation required them to cherish enmity toward the Samaritans. They wondered at the conduct of Jesus. They could not refuse to follow His example, and during the two days in Samaria, fidelity to Him kept their prejudices under control; yet in heart they were unreconciled. They were slow to learn that their contempt and hatred must give place to pity and sympathy. But after the Lord's ascension, His lessons came back to them with a new meaning. After the outpouring of the Holy Spirit, they recalled the Saviour's look, His words, the respect and tenderness of His bearing toward these despised strangers. When Peter went to preach in Samaria, he brought the same spirit into his own work. When John was called to Ephesus and Smyrna, he remembered the experience at Shechem, and was filled with gratitude to the divine Teacher, who, foreseeing the difficulties they must meet, had given them help in His own example. *Desire of Ages,* 193.

Peter had come to Christ with the question, "How oft shall my brother sin against me, and I forgive him? till seven times?" The rabbis limited the exercise of forgiveness to three offenses. Peter, carrying out, as he supposed, the teaching of Christ, thought to extend it to seven, the number signifying perfection. But Christ taught that we are never to become weary of forgiving. Not "Until seven times," He said, "but, Until seventy times seven." *Christ's Object Lessons,* 243.

The great reason why so many professed disciples of Christ fall into grievous temptation and make work for repentance is that they are deficient in a knowledge of themselves. Here is where Peter was so thoroughly sifted by the enemy. Here is where thousands will make shipwreck of faith. You do not take your wrongs and errors to heart, and afflict your souls over them. I entreat you to purify your souls by obeying the truth. Connect yourselves with heaven. And may the Lord save you from self-deception. *Testimonies for the Church*, Volume 4, 246.

And not all, even of those who appear most faulty, are like Judas. Peter, impetuous, hasty, and self-confident, often appeared to far greater disadvantage than Judas did. He was oftener reproved by the Saviour. But what a life of service and sacrifice was his! What a testimony does it bear to the power of God's grace! So far as we are capable, we are to be to others what Jesus was to His disciples when He walked and talked with them on the earth. *Ministry of Healing*, 493.

Peter, impetuous, hasty, and self-confident, often appeared to far greater disadvantage than Judas did.

When Jesus sent His disciples forth to labor, . . . they did not feel as some do now, that they would rather work alone than have anyone with them who did not labor just as they labored. Our Saviour understood what ones to associate together. He did not connect with the mild, beloved John one of the same temperament; but He connected with him the ardent, impulsive Peter. These two men were not alike either in their disposition or in their manner of labor. Peter was prompt and zealous in action, bold and uncompromising, and would often wound; John was ever calm, and considerate of others' feelings, and would come after to bind up and encourage. Thus the defects in one were partially covered by the virtues in the other. *Evangelism*, 72.

I was then carried back to the days of the apostles and saw that God chose as companions an ardent, zealous Peter and a mild, patient John. Sometimes Peter was impetuous, and often when this was the case the beloved disciple would check him. This, however, did not reform him. But after he had denied his Lord, repented, and been converted, all he needed to check his ardor and zeal was a mild caution from John. The cause of Christ would often have suffered had it been left to John alone. Peter's zeal was needed. His boldness and energy often delivered them from difficulty and silenced their enemies. John was winning. He gained many to the cause of Christ by his patient forbearance and deep devotedness. *Early Writings,* 224.

When Peter said he would follow his Lord to prison and to death, he meant it, every word of it; but he did not know himself. Hidden in his heart were elements of evil that circumstances would fan into life. Unless he was made conscious of his danger, these would prove his eternal ruin. The Saviour saw in him a self-love and assurance that would overbear even his love for Christ. Much of infirmity, of unmortified sin, carelessness of spirit, unsanctified temper, heedlessness in entering into temptation, had been revealed in his experience. Christ's solemn warning was a call to heart searching. Peter needed to distrust himself, and to have a deeper faith in Christ. Had he in humility received the warning, he would have appealed to the Shepherd of the flock to keep His sheep. When on the Sea of Galilee he was about to sink, he cried, "Lord, save me." Matthew 14:30. Then the hand of Christ was outstretched to grasp his hand. So now if he had cried to Jesus, Save me from myself, he would have been kept. But Peter felt that he was distrusted, and he thought it cruel. He was already offended, and he became more persistent in his self-confidence. *Desire of Ages*, 673.

Peter had not designed that his real character should be known. In assuming an air of indifference he had placed himself on the enemy's ground, and he became an easy prey to temptation. If he had been called to fight for his Master, he would have been a courageous soldier; but when the finger of scorn was pointed at him, he proved himself a coward. Many who do not shrink from active warfare for their Lord are driven by ridicule to deny their faith. By associating with those whom they should avoid, they place themselves in the way of temptation. They invite the enemy to tempt them, and are led to say and do that of which under other circumstances they would never have been guilty. The disciple of Christ who in our day disguises his faith through dread of suffering or reproach denies his Lord as really as did Peter in the judgment hall. *Desire of Ages,* 712.

For each of the classes represented by the Pharisee and the publican there is a lesson in the history of the apostle Peter. In his early discipleship Peter thought himself strong. Like the Pharisee, in his own estimation he was "not as other men are." When Christ on the eve of His betrayal forewarned His disciples, "All ye shall be offended because of Me this night," Peter confidently declared, "Although all shall be offended, yet will not I." Mark 14:27, 29. Peter did not know his own danger. Self-confidence misled him. He thought himself able to withstand temptation; but in a few short hours the test came, and with cursing and swearing he denied his Lord. *Christ's Object Lessons*, 152.

As Peter walked beside Jesus, he saw that John was following. A desire came over him to know his future, and he "saith to Jesus, Lord, and what shall this man do? Jesus saith unto him, If I will that he tarry till I come, what is that to thee? follow thou Me." Peter should have considered that his Lord would reveal to him all that it was best for him to know. It is the duty of everyone to follow Christ, without undue anxiety as to the work assigned to others. In saying of John, "If I will that he tarry till I come," Jesus gave no assurance that this disciple should live until the Lord's second coming. He merely asserted His own supreme power, and that even if He should will this to be so, it would in no way affect Peter's work. The future of both John and Peter was in the hands of their Lord. Obedience in following Him was the duty required of each.

How many today are like Peter! They are interested in the affairs of others, and anxious to know their duty, while they are in danger of neglecting their own. It is our work to look to Christ and follow Him. We shall see mistakes in the lives of others, and defects in their character. Humanity is encompassed with infirmity. But in Christ we shall find perfection. Beholding Him, we shall become transformed. *Desire of Ages,* 816.

The Stone and the Rock

When he again joined his disciples, he asked them: "Whom do men say that I, the Son of Man, am? And they said, Some say that thou art John the Baptist; some, Elias; and others, Jeremias, or one of the prophets." Questioning still closer, he inquired, "But whom say ye that I am?" Peter, ever ready to speak, answered for himself and his brethren: "Thou art Christ, the Son of the living God. And Jesus answered and said unto him, Blessed art thou, Simon Bar-jona; for flesh and blood hath not revealed it unto thee, but my Father which is in Heaven." Notwithstanding the faith of many had utterly failed, and the power of the priests and rulers was mighty against them, the brave disciple thus boldly declared his belief. Jesus saw, in this acknowledgment, the living principle that would animate the hearts of his believers in coming ages. It is the mysterious working of God's Spirit upon the human heart, that elevates the humblest mind to a knowledge above all earthly wisdom, an acquaintance with the sacred truths of God. Ah, indeed, "blessed art thou, Simon Barjona, for flesh and blood hath not revealed it unto thee."

Jesus continued: "And I say also unto thee, That thou art Peter, and upon this rock I will build my church; and the gates of hell shall not prevail against it." The word Peter signifies rolling stone. Christ did not refer to Peter as being the rock upon which he would found his church. His expression, "this rock," applied to himself as the foundation of the Christian church. In Isaiah 28:16, the same reference is made: "Therefore thus saith the Lord God, Behold, I lay in Zion, for a foundation, a stone, a tried stone, a precious corner stone, a sure foundation." It is the same stone to which reference is made in Luke 20:17, 18: "And he beheld them, and said, What is this then that is written, The stone which the builders rejected, the same is become the head of the corner? Whosoever shall fall upon that stone shall be broken; but on whomsoever it shall fall, it will grind him to powder." Also in Mark 12:10, 11: "And have ye not read this scripture, The stone which the builders rejected is become the head of the corner. This was the Lord's doing, and it is marvelous in our eyes?"

These texts prove conclusively that Christ is the rock upon which the church is built, and, in his address to Peter, he referred to himself as the rock which is the foundation of the church. *Redemption: Or the Miracles of Christ, the Mighty One,* (1877), 65, 66.

Peter had expressed the faith of the twelve. Yet the disciples were still far from understanding Christ's mission. The opposition and misrepresentation of the priests and rulers, while it could not turn them away from Christ, still caused them great perplexity. They did not see their way clearly. The influence of their early training, the teaching of the rabbis, the power of tradition, still intercepted their view of truth. From time to time precious rays of light from Jesus shone upon them, yet often they were like men groping among shadows. But on this day, before they were brought face to face with the great trial of their faith, the Holy Spirit rested upon them in power. For a little time their eyes were turned away from "the things which are seen," to behold "the things which are not seen." 2 Corinthians 4:18. Beneath the guise of humanity they discerned the glory of the Son of God.

From time to time precious rays of light from Jesus shone upon them, yet often they were like men groping among shadows.

Jesus answered Peter, saying, "Blessed art thou, Simon Bar-jona: for flesh and blood hath not revealed it unto thee, but My Father which is in heaven."

The truth which Peter had confessed is the foundation of the believer's faith. It is that which Christ Himself has declared to be eternal life. But the possession of this knowledge was no ground for self-glorification. Through no wisdom or goodness of his own had it been revealed to Peter. Never can humanity, of itself, attain to a knowledge of the divine. "It is as high as heaven; what canst thou do? deeper than hell; what canst thou know?" Job 11:8. Only the spirit of adoption can reveal to us the deep things of God, which "eye hath not seen, nor ear heard, neither have entered into the heart of man." "God hath revealed them unto us by His Spirit: for the Spirit searcheth all things, yea, the deep things of God." 1 Corinthians 2:9, 10. "The secret of the Lord is with them that fear Him;" and the fact that Peter discerned the glory of Christ was an evidence that he had been "taught of God." Psalm 25:14; John 6:45. Ah, indeed, "blessed art thou, Simon Bar-jona: for flesh and blood hath not revealed it unto thee."

Jesus continued: "I say also unto thee, That thou art Peter, and upon this rock I will build My church; and the gates of hell shall not prevail against it." The word Peter signifies a stone,--a rolling stone. Peter was not the rock upon which the church was founded. The gates of hell did prevail against him when he denied his Lord with cursing and swearing. The church was built upon One against whom the gates of hell could not prevail. *Desire of Ages*, 412.

The heart of Peter had been touched by the Holy Spirit of God. Rays of light from heaven had flashed into his soul and warmed his heart with love for Christ. Jesus was acknowledged as well as known as the Messiah so earnestly looked for by the Jewish nation. "And Jesus answered and said unto him, Blessed art thou, Simon Bar-jona; for flesh and blood hath not revealed it unto thee, but My Father which is in heaven."

In His answer, Christ did not exalt Peter above his breth-ren, nor give him superiority over his fellow apostles. He did not address Peter alone, but the established Christian church. To Peter He said, "Thou art Peter"--by interpretation a stone-- then, turning to His disciples, He said, "On this rock," referring to Himself, "I will build My church; and the gates of hell shall not prevail against it."

It was not the purpose of Christ to exalt one above another. In all His teachings He sought to lead His disciples to humility of heart. "Learn of Me," He said; "for I am meek and lowly in heart; and ye shall find rest unto your souls." Had Peter felt the necessity of taking the lessons of Christ more fully to heart; had he learned the meekness and lowliness of Christ, he would have saved him- self sorrow which left its impress upon his memory as long as life lasted. *Signs of the Times,* August 11, 1898.

Peter had expressed the truth which is the foundation of the church's faith, and Jesus now honored him as the representative of the whole body of believers. He said, "I will give unto thee the keys of the kingdom of heaven: and whatsoever thou shalt bind on earth shall be bound in heaven: and whatsoever thou shalt loose on earth shall be loosed in heaven."

"The keys of the kingdom of heaven" are the words of Christ. All the words of Holy Scripture are His, and are here included. These words have power to open and to shut heaven. They declare the conditions upon which men are received or rejected. Thus the work of those who preach God's word is a savor of life unto life or of death unto death. Theirs is a mission weighted with eternal results.

The Saviour did not commit the work of the gospel to Peter individually. At a later time, repeating the words that were spoken to Peter, He applied them directly to the church. And the same in substance was spoken also to the twelve as representatives of the body of believers. If Jesus had delegated any special authority to one of the disciples above the others, we should not find them so often contending as to who should be the greatest. They would have submitted to the wish of their Master, and honored the one whom He had chosen. *Desire of Ages,* 413, 414.

Walking on Water

At the moment when they believe themselves lost, a gleam of light reveals a mysterious figure approaching them upon the water. But they know not that it is Jesus. The One who has come for their help they count as an enemy. Terror overpowers them. The hands that have grasped the oars with muscles like iron let go their hold. The boat rocks at the will of the waves; all eyes are riveted on this vision of a man walking upon the white-capped billows of the foaming sea.

They think it a phantom that omens their destruction, and they cry out for fear. Jesus advances as if He would pass them; but they recognize Him, and cry out, entreating His help. Their beloved Master turns, His voice silences their fear, "Be of good cheer: it is I; be not afraid."

As soon as they could credit the wondrous fact, Peter was almost beside himself with joy. As if he could scarcely yet believe, he cried out, "Lord, if it be Thou, bid me come unto Thee on the water. And He said, Come."

Looking unto Jesus, Peter walks securely; but as in self-satisfaction he glances back toward his companions in the boat, his eyes are turned from the Saviour. The wind is boisterous. The waves roll high, and come directly between him and the Master; and he is afraid. For a moment Christ is hidden from his view, and his faith gives way. He begins to sink. But while the billows talk with death, Peter lifts his eyes from the angry waters, and fixing them upon Jesus, cries, "Lord, save me." Immediately Jesus grasps the outstretched hand, saying, "O thou of little faith, wherefore didst thou doubt?"

Walking side by side, Peter's hand in that of his Master, they stepped into the boat together. But Peter was now subdued and silent. He had no reason to boast over his fellows, for through unbelief and self-exaltation he had very nearly lost his life. When he turned his eyes from Jesus, his footing was lost, and he sank amid the waves.

When trouble comes upon us, how often we are like Peter! We look upon the waves, instead of keeping our eyes fixed upon the Saviour. Our footsteps slide, and the proud waters go over our souls. Jesus did not bid Peter come to Him that he should perish; He does not call us to follow Him, and then forsake us. "Fear not," He says; "for I have redeemed thee, I have called thee by thy name; thou art Mine. When thou passest through the waters, I will be with thee; and through the rivers, they shall not overflow thee: when thou walkest through the fire, thou shalt not be burned; neither shall the flame kindle upon thee. For I am the Lord thy God, the Holy One of Israel, thy Saviour." Isaiah 43:1-3. *Desire of Ages*, 381-382.

This incident illustrates much of the character of impulsive Peter. Faith and unbelief were blended in his words and actions. He said, "Lord, if it be thou, bid me come unto thee on the water." The Lord had assured the disciples, "It is I; be not afraid." And when Peter saw the waves around him, saw the boisterous winds, he forgot the power of his Lord, and began to sink; but at his cry of weakness, Jesus was at his side to grasp his outstretched hand, and lift him from the billows. *Review and Herald,* April 7, 1891.

Peter Before the Tax Collector

Soon after they reached the town, the collector of the temple revenue came to Peter with the question, "Doth not your Master pay tribute?" This tribute was not a civil tax, but a religious contribution, which every Jew was required to pay annually for the support of the temple. A refusal to pay the tribute would be regarded as disloyalty to the temple,--in the estimation of the rabbis a most grievous sin. The Saviour's attitude toward the rabbinical laws, and His plain reproofs to the defenders of tradition, afforded a pretext for the charge that He was seeking to overthrow the temple service. Now His enemies saw an opportunity of casting discredit upon Him. In the collector of the tribute they found a ready ally.

Peter saw in the collector's question an insinuation touching Christ's loyalty to the temple. Zealous for his Master's honor, he hastily answered, without consulting Him, that Jesus would pay the tribute.

But Peter only partially comprehended the purpose of his questioner. There were some classes who were held to be exempt from the payment of the tribute. In the time of Moses, when the Levites were set apart for the service of the sanctuary, they were given no inheritance among the people. The Lord said, "Levi hath no part nor inheritance with his brethren; the Lord is his inheritance." Deuteronomy 10:9. In the days of Christ the priests and Levites were still regarded as especially devoted to the temple, and were not required to make the annual contribution for its support. Prophets also were exempted from this payment. In requiring the tribute from Jesus, the rabbis were setting aside His claim as a prophet or teacher, and were dealing with Him as with any commonplace person. A refusal on His part to pay the tribute would be represented as disloyalty to the temple; while, on the other hand, the payment of it would be taken as justifying their rejection of Him as a prophet.

Only a little before, Peter had acknowledged Jesus as the Son of God; but he now missed an opportunity of setting forth the character of his Master. By his answer to the collector, that Jesus would pay the tribute, he had virtually sanctioned the false conception of Him to which the priests and rulers were trying to give currency. *Desire of Ages*, 432, 433.

Chapter Two

Hard Lessons

"Get Thee Behind Me, Satan"

When the Lord sought to prepare the minds of his disciples for their last great trial in his betrayal and crucifixion, Peter felt that he could not bear to have the words of the Lord fulfilled; and stirred with indignation at the thought of the injustice so soon to come upon Christ and his followers, he exclaimed, "Be it far from thee, Lord; this shall not be unto thee." The impression which Christ desired to make upon the minds of his followers was one directly opposed to the impression that Peter's words would make, and he rebuked his disciple with the sternest rebuke that ever fell from his lips. He said, "Get thee behind me, Satan: thou art an offense unto me; for thou savorest not the things that be of God; but those that be of men."

Although Peter had been long with the Master, he had a very imperfect conception of the plan of salvation. He did not desire to see the cross in the work of Christ; but it was through the cross that life and hope were to come to dying men.

When Jesus had spoken of his death, declaring that all his disciples would be offended because of him, Peter had said, "Though all men shall be offended because of thee, yet will I never be offended." He assured his Lord that he would go with him both to prison and to death; but Jesus knew Peter much better than the disciple knew himself, and he said to him, "Verily I say unto thee, That this night, before the cock crow, thou shalt deny me thrice." *Review and Herald*, April 7, 1891.

When Christ revealed to Peter the time of trial and suffering that was just before Him, and Peter replied, "Be it far from thee, Lord: this shall not be unto thee" (Matthew 16:22), the Saviour commanded, "Get thee behind me, Satan" (Matthew 16:23). Satan was speaking through Peter, making him act the part of the tempter. Satan's presence was unsuspected by Peter, but Christ could detect the presence of the deceiver, and in His rebuke to Peter He addressed the real foe. *Selected Messages,* Volume 2, 353.

Satan was speaking through Peter, making him act the part of the tempter. Satan's presence was unsuspected by Peter, but Christ could detect the presence of the deceiver, and in His rebuke to Peter He addressed the real foe.

Satan's work was to discourage Jesus as He strove to save the depraved race, and Peter's words were just what he wished to hear. They were opposed to the divine plan; and whatever bore this stamp of character was an offense to God. They were spoken at the instigation of Satan; for they opposed the only arrangement God could make to preserve His law and control His subjects, and yet save fallen man. Satan hoped they would discourage and dishearten Christ; but Christ addressed the author of the thought, saying, "Get thee behind me, Satan" *Review and Herald,* April 6, 1897.

The disciples had thought that their Master would not suffer Himself to be taken. For the same power that had caused the mob to fall as dead men could keep them helpless, until Jesus and His companions should escape. They were disappointed and indignant as they saw the cords brought forward to bind the hands of Him whom they loved. Peter in his anger rashly drew his sword and tried to defend his Master, but he only cut off an ear of the high priest's servant. When Jesus saw what was done, He released His hands, though held firmly by the Roman soldiers, and saying, "Suffer ye thus far," He touched the wounded ear, and it was instantly made whole. He then said to Peter, "Put up again thy sword into his place: for all they that take the sword shall perish with the sword. Thinkest thou that I cannot now pray to My Father, and He shall presently give Me more than twelve legions of angels?"--a legion in place of each one of the disciples. Oh, why, the disciples thought, does He not save Himself and us? Answering their unspoken thought, He added, "But how then shall the scriptures be fulfilled, that thus it must be?" "The cup which My Father hath given Me, shall I not drink it?" …

The disciples were terrified as they saw Jesus permit Himself to be taken and bound. They were offended that He should suffer this humiliation to Himself and them. They could not understand His conduct, and they blamed Him for submitting to the mob. In their indignation and fear, Peter proposed that they save themselves. Following this suggestion, "they all forsook Him, and fled." But Christ had foretold this desertion, "Behold," He had said, "the hour cometh, yea, is now come, that ye shall be scattered, every man to his own, and shall leave Me alone: and yet I am not alone, because the Father is with Me." John 16:32. *Desire of Ages*, 696, 697.

Peter's Denial of Christ

After the hymn, they went out. Through the crowded streets they made their way, passing out of the city gate toward the Mount of Olives. Slowly they proceeded, each busy with his own thoughts. As they began to descend toward the mount, Jesus said, in a tone of deepest sadness, "All ye shall be offended because of Me this night: for it is written, I will smite the shepherd, and the sheep of the flock shall be scattered abroad." Matthew 26:31. The disciples listened in sorrow and amazement. They remembered how in the synagogue at Capernaum, when Christ spoke of Himself as the bread of life, many had been offended, and had turned away from Him. But the twelve had not shown themselves unfaithful. Peter, speaking for his brethren, had then declared his loyalty to Christ. Then the Saviour had said, "Have not I chosen you twelve, and one of you is a devil?" John 6:70. In the upper chamber Jesus said that one of the twelve would betray Him, and that Peter would deny Him. But now His words include them all.

Now Peter's voice is heard vehemently protesting, "Although all shall be offended, yet will not I." In the upper chamber he had declared, "I will lay down my life for Thy sake." Jesus had warned him that he would that very night deny his Saviour. Now Christ repeats the warning: "Verily I say unto thee, That this day, even in this night, before the cock crow twice, thou shalt deny Me thrice." But Peter only "spake the more vehemently, If I should die with Thee, I will not deny Thee in anywise. Likewise also said they all." Mark 14:29, 30, 31. In their self-confidence they denied the repeated statement of Him who knew. They were unprepared for the test; when temptation should overtake them, they would understand their own weakness. *Desire of Ages*, 673.

Do not act from motives of policy. The great danger of our businessmen and those in responsible positions is that they will be turned from Christ to secure some help aside from Him. Peter would not have been left to show such weakness and folly had he not sought by the use of policy to avoid reproach and scorn, persecution and abuse. His highest hopes centered in Christ; but when he saw Him in humiliation, unbelief came in and was entertained.

He fell under the power of temptation, and, instead of showing his fidelity in a crisis, he wickedly denied his Lord. *Testimonies for the Church*, Volume 5, 427.

Peter's fall was not instantaneous, but gradual. Self-confidence led him to the belief that he was saved, and step after step was taken in the downward path, until he could deny his Master. Never can we safely put confidence in self or feel, this side of heaven, that we are secure against temptation. Those who accept the Saviour, however sincere their conversion, should never be taught to say or to feel that they are saved. This is misleading. Every one should be taught to cherish hope and faith; but even when we give ourselves to Christ and know that He accepts us, we are not beyond the reach of temptation. God's word declares, "Many shall be purified, and made white, and tried." Daniel 12:10. Only he who endures the trial will receive the crown of life. (James 1:12.)

The evil that led to Peter's fall and that shut out the Pharisee from communion with God is proving the ruin of thousands today. There is nothing so offensive to God or so dangerous to the human soul as pride and self-sufficiency. Of all sins it is the most hopeless, the most incurable. *Christ's Object Lessons*, 154, 155.

Never was criminal treated in so inhuman a manner as was the Son of God.

But a keener anguish rent the heart of Jesus; the blow that inflicted the deepest pain no enemy's hand could have dealt. While He was undergoing the mockery of an examination before Caiaphas, Christ had been denied by one of His own disciples.

After deserting their Master in the garden, two of the disciples had ventured to follow, at a distance, the mob that had Jesus in charge. These disciples were Peter and John. The priests recognized John as a well-known disciple of Jesus, and admitted him to the hall, hoping that as he witnessed the humiliation of his Leader, he would scorn the idea of such a one being the Son of God. John spoke in favor of Peter, and gained an entrance for him also.

In the court a fire had been kindled; for it was the coldest hour of the night, being just before the dawn. A company drew about the fire, and Peter presumptuously took his place with them. He did not wish to be recognized as a disciple of Jesus. By mingling carelessly with the crowd, he hoped to be taken for one of those who had brought Jesus to the hall.

But as the light flashed upon Peter's face, the woman who kept the door cast a searching glance upon him. She had noticed that he came in with John, she marked the look of dejection on his face, and thought that he might be a disciple of Jesus. She was one of the servants of Caiaphas' household, and was curious to know. She said to Peter, "Art not thou also one of this Man's disciples?" Peter was startled and confused; the eyes of the company instantly fastened upon him. He pretended not to understand her; but she was persistent, and said to those around her that this man was with Jesus. Peter felt compelled to answer, and said angrily, "Woman, I know Him not." This was the first denial, and immediately the cock crew. O Peter, so soon ashamed of thy Master! so soon to deny thy Lord!

The disciple John, upon entering the judgment hall, did not try to conceal the fact that he was a follower of Jesus. He did not mingle with the rough company who were reviling his Master. He was not questioned, for he did not assume a false character, and thus lay himself liable to suspicion. He sought a retired corner secure from the notice of the mob, but as near Jesus as it was possible for him to be. Here he could see and hear all that took place at the trial of his Lord.

Peter had not designed that his real character should be known. In assuming an air of indifference he had placed himself on the enemy's ground, and he became an easy prey to temptation. If he had been called to fight for his Master, he would have been a courageous soldier; but when the finger of scorn was pointed at him, he proved himself a coward. Many who do not shrink from active warfare for their Lord are driven by ridicule to deny their faith. By associating with those whom they should avoid, they place themselves in the way of temptation. They invite the enemy to tempt them, and are led to say and do that of which under other circumstances they would never have been guilty. The disciple of Christ who in our day disguises his faith through dread of suffering or reproach denies his Lord as really as did Peter in the judgment hall.

Many who do not shrink from active warfare for their Lord are driven by ridicule to deny their faith. By associating with those whom they should avoid, they place themselves in the way of temptation.

Peter tried to show no interest in the trial of his Master, but his heart was wrung with sorrow as he heard the cruel taunts, and saw the abuse He was suffering. More than this, he was surprised and angry that Jesus should humiliate Himself and His followers by submitting to such treatment. In order to conceal his true feelings, he endeavored to join with the persecutors of Jesus in their untimely jests. But his appearance was unnatural. He was acting a lie, and while seeking to talk unconcernedly he could not restrain expressions of indignation at the abuse heaped upon his Master.

Attention was called to him the second time, and he was again charged with being a follower of Jesus. He now declared with an oath, "I do not know the Man." Still another opportunity was given him. An hour had passed, when one of the servants of the high priest, being a near kinsman of the man whose ear Peter had cut off, asked him, "Did not I see thee in the garden with Him?" "Surely thou art one of them: for thou art a Galilean, and thy speech agreeth thereto." At this Peter flew into a rage. The disciples of Jesus were noted for the purity of their language, and in order fully to deceive his questioners, and justify his assumed character, Peter now denied his Master with cursing and swearing. Again the cock crew. Peter heard it then, and he remembered the words of Jesus, "Before the cock crow twice, thou shalt deny Me thrice." Mark 14:30.

While the degrading oaths were fresh upon Peter's lips, and the shrill crowing of the cock was still ringing in his ears, the Saviour turned from the frowning judges, and looked full upon His poor disciple. At the same time Peter's eyes were drawn to his Master. In that gentle countenance he read deep pity and sorrow, but there was no anger there.

The sight of that pale, suffering face, those quivering lips, that look of compassion and forgiveness, pierced his heart like an arrow. Conscience was aroused. Memory was active. Peter called to mind his promise of a few short hours before that he would go with his Lord to prison and to death. He remembered his grief when the Saviour told him in the upper chamber that he would deny his Lord thrice that same night. Peter had just declared that he knew not Jesus, but he now realized with bitter grief how well his Lord knew him, and how accurately He had read his heart, the falseness of which was unknown even to himself. *Desire of Ages*, 710-713.

Peter's Bitter Remorse

A tide of memories rushed over him. The Saviour's tender mercy, His kindness and long-suffering, His gentleness and patience toward His erring disciples,--all was remembered. He recalled the caution, "Simon, behold, Satan hath desired to have you, that he may sift you as wheat: but I have prayed for thee, that thy faith fail not." Luke 22:31, 32. He reflected with horror upon his own ingratitude, his falsehood, his perjury. Once more he looked at his Master, and saw a sacrilegious hand raised to smite Him in the face. Unable longer to endure the scene, he rushed, heartbroken, from the hall.

He pressed on in solitude and darkness, he knew not and cared not whither. At last he found himself in Gethsemane. The scene of a few hours before came vividly to his mind. The suffering face of his Lord, stained with bloody sweat and convulsed with anguish, rose before him. He remembered with bitter remorse that Jesus had wept and agonized in prayer alone, while those who should have united with Him in that trying hour were sleeping. He remembered His solemn charge, "Watch and pray, that ye enter not into temptation." Matthew 26:41. He witnessed again the scene in the judgment hall. It was torture to his bleeding heart to know that he had added the heaviest burden to the Saviour's humiliation and grief. On the very spot where Jesus had poured out His soul in agony to His Father, Peter fell upon his face, and wished that he might die.

It was in sleeping when Jesus bade him watch and pray that Peter had prepared the way for his great sin. All the disciples, by sleeping in that critical hour, sustained a great loss. Christ knew the fiery ordeal through which they were to pass. He knew how Satan would work to paralyze their senses that they might be unready for the trial. Therefore it was that He gave them warning. Had those hours in the garden been spent in watching and prayer, Peter would not have been left to depend upon his own feeble strength. He would not have denied his Lord. Had the disciples watched with Christ in His agony, they would have been prepared to behold His suffering upon the cross. They would have understood in some degree the nature of His overpowering anguish. They would have been able to recall His words that foretold His sufferings, His death, and His resurrection. Amid the gloom of the most trying hour, some rays of hope would have lighted up the darkness and sustained their faith. *Desire of Ages*, 713.

Satan was permitted to tempt the too confident Peter, as he had been permitted to tempt Job; but when that work was done, he had to retire. Had Satan been suffered to have his way, there would have been no hope for Peter.

Satan was permitted to tempt the too confident Peter, as he had been permitted to tempt Job; but when that work was done, he had to retire. Had Satan been suffered to have his way, there would have been no hope for Peter. He would have made complete shipwreck of faith. But the enemy dare not go one hair's-breadth beyond his appointed sphere. There is no power in the whole satanic force that can disable the soul that trusts, in simple confidence, in the wisdom that comes from God. *The Youth's Instructor*, December 15, 1898.

It was to the disciple a bitter lesson, and one which he learned but slowly, that the path of Christ on earth lay through agony and humiliation. But in the heat of the furnace fire he was to learn its lesson. Now, when his once active form was bowed with the burden of years and labors, he could write, "Beloved, think it not strange concerning the fiery trial which is to try you, as though some strange thing happened unto you: but rejoice, inasmuch as ye are partakers of Christ's sufferings; that, when His glory shall be revealed, ye may be glad also with exceeding joy." *Acts of the Apostles*, 525.

Chapter Three

A New Man in Christ

Peter denied the Man of Sorrows in His acquaintance with grief in the hour of His humiliation. But he afterward repented and was reconverted. He had true contrition of soul and gave himself afresh to his Saviour. With blinding tears he makes his way to the solitudes of the Garden of Gethsemane and there prostrates himself where he saw his Saviour's prostrate form when the bloody sweat was forced from His pores by His great agony. Peter remembers with remorse that he was asleep when Jesus prayed during those fearful hours. His proud heart breaks, and penitential tears moisten the sods so recently stained with the bloody sweat drops of God's dear Son. He left that garden a converted man. He was ready then to pity the tempted. He was humbled and could sympathize with the weak and erring. He could caution and warn the presumptuous, and was fully fitted to strengthen his brethren. *Testimonies for the Church*, Volume 3, 416.

[H]aving the same spirit which Peter possessed after his apostasy, you will be victors. He felt a sense of his cowardly denial of Christ throughout his lifetime; and when called to suffer martyrdom for his faith, this humiliating fact was ever before him, and he begged that he might not be crucified in the exact manner in which his Lord suffered, fearing that it would be too great an honor after his apostasy. His request was that he might be crucified with his head downward. What a sense did Peter have of his sin in denying his Lord! What a conversion he experienced! His life ever after was a life of repentance and humiliation. *Testimonies for the Church*, Volume 4, 342.

"Lovest Thou Me?"

The disciples expected that Peter would no longer be allowed to occupy the prominent position in the work which he had hitherto held, and he himself had lost his customary self-confidence. But Jesus, while dining by the sea-side, singled out Peter, saying, "Simon, son of Jonas, lovest thou me more than these?" referring to his brethren. Peter had once said, "Though all men shall be offended because of thee, yet will I never be offended," and had expressed himself ready to go to prison and to death with his Master. But now he puts a true estimate upon himself in the presence of the disciples: "Yea, Lord, thou knowest that I love thee." In this response of Peter there is no vehement assurance that his affection is greater than that of his companions; he does not even express his own opinion of his devotion to his Saviour, but appeals to that Saviour, who can read all the motives of the human heart, to himself judge as to his sincerity,--"Thou knowest that I love thee." *The Spirit of Prophecy*, Volume 3, 229.

While Christ and the disciples were eating together by the sea-side, the Saviour said to Peter, "Simon, son of Jonas, lovest thou Me more than these?" referring to his brethren. Peter had once declared, "Though all men shall be offended because of Thee, yet will I never be offended." Matthew 26:33. But he now put a truer estimate upon himself. "Yea, Lord," he said, "Thou knowest that I love Thee." There is no vehement assurance that his love is greater than that of his brethren. He does not express his own opinion of his devotion. To Him who can read all the motives of the heart he appeals to judge as to his sincerity,--"Thou knowest that I love Thee." And Jesus bids him, "Feed My lambs."

Again Jesus applied the test to Peter, repeating His former words: "Simon, son of Jonas, lovest thou Me?" This time He did not ask Peter whether he loved Him better than did his brethren. The second response was like the first, free from extravagant assurance: "Yea, Lord; Thou knowest that I love Thee." Jesus said to him, "Feed My sheep." Once more the Saviour put the trying question: "Simon, son of Jonas, lovest thou Me?" Peter was grieved; he thought that Jesus doubted his love. He knew that his Lord had cause to distrust him, and with an aching heart he answered, "Lord, Thou knowest all things; Thou knowest that I love Thee." Again Jesus said to him, "Feed My sheep."

Three times Peter had openly denied his Lord, and three times Jesus drew from him the assurance of his love and loyalty, pressing home that pointed question, like a barbed arrow to his wounded heart. Before the assembled disciples Jesus revealed the depth of Peter's repentance, and showed how thoroughly humbled was the once boasting disciple.

Peter was naturally forward and impulsive, and Satan had taken advantage of these characteristics to overthrow him. Just before the fall of Peter, Jesus had said to him, "Satan hath desired to have you, that he may sift you as wheat: but I have prayed for thee, that thy faith fail not: and when thou art converted, strengthen thy brethren." Luke 22:31, 32. That time had now come, and the transformation in Peter was evident. The close, testing questions of the Lord had not called out one forward, self-sufficient reply; and because of his humiliation and repentance, Peter was better prepared than ever before to act as shepherd to the flock. *Desire of Ages*, 811, 812.

There was Peter, who denied his Lord. After he had fallen and been converted, Jesus said to him, "Feed my lambs." Before Peter's feet slipped, he had not the spirit of meekness required to feed the lambs; but after he became sensible of his own weakness, he knew just how to teach the erring and fallen; he could come close to their side in tender sympathy, and could help them. *SDA Bible Commentary,* Volume 5, 1151.

Peter never forgot the painful scene of his humiliation. He did not forget his denial of Christ, and think that, after all, it was not a very great sin. All was painfully real to the erring disciple. His sorrow for his sin was as intense as had been his denial. After his conversion, the old assertions were not made in the old spirit and manner.

No restoration can be complete unless it reaches to the very depth of the soul by the transforming power of the Holy Spirit. Under the Holy Spirit's influence, Peter stood before a congregation of thousands, and in holy boldness charged the wicked priests and rulers with the very sin of which he himself had been guilty. "Ye denied the Holy One and the Just," he said, "and desired a murderer to be granted unto you; and killed the Prince of life, whom God hath raised from the dead; whereof we are witnesses. . . . And now, brethren, I wot that through ignorance ye did it, as did also your rulers. But those things, which God before had showed by the mouth of all his prophets, that Christ should suffer, he hath so fulfilled." There was now no moral insensibility upon Peter. As Christ's witness, under the inspiration of the Spirit of God, he gave evidence of his divine restoration.

Three times after his resurrection, Christ tested Peter. "Simon, son of Jonas," he said, "lovest thou me more than these? He saith unto him, Yea, Lord; thou knowest that I love thee. He saith unto him, Feed my lambs. He saith to him again the second time, Simon, son of Jonas, lovest thou me? He saith unto him, Yea, Lord; thou knowest that I love thee. He saith unto him, Feed my sheep."

This heart-searching question was necessary in the case of Peter, and it is necessary in our case. The work of restoration can never be thorough unless the roots of evil are reached. Again and again the shoots have been clipped, while the root of bitterness has been left to spring up and defile many; but the very depth of the hidden evil must be reached, the moral senses must be judged, and judged again, in the light of the divine presence. The daily life will testify whether or not the work is genuine.

When, the third time, Christ said to Peter, "Lovest thou me?" the probe reached the soul center. Self-judged, Peter fell upon the Rock, saying, "Lord, thou knowest all things; thou knowest that I love thee."

This is the work before every soul who has dishonored God, and grieved the heart of Christ, by a denial of truth and righteousness. If the tempted soul endures the trying process, and self does not awake to life to feel hurt and abused under the test, that probing knife reveals that the soul is indeed dead to self, but alive unto God.

Christ gave to Peter the strongest evidence of his confidence in his restoration. And he was commissioned to feed not only the sheep, but the lambs,—a broader and more delicate work than had hitherto been appointed him.

Some assert that if a soul stumbles and falls, he can never regain his position; but the case before us contradicts this. Before his denial, Christ said to Peter, "When thou art converted, strengthen thy brethren." In committing to his stewardship the souls for whom he had given his life, Christ gave to Peter the strongest evidence of his confidence in his restoration. And he was commissioned to feed not only the sheep, but the lambs,--a broader and more delicate work than had hitherto been appointed him. Not only was he to hold forth the word of life to others, but he was to be a shepherd of the flock. *The Youth's Instructor*, December 22, 1898.

The question that Christ had put to Peter was significant. He mentioned only one condition of discipleship and service. "Lovest thou Me?" He said. This is the essential qualification. Though Peter might possess every other, yet without the love of Christ he could not be a faithful shepherd over the Lord's flock. Knowledge, benevolence, eloquence, gratitude, and zeal are all aids in the good work; but without the love of Jesus in the heart, the work of the Christian minister is a failure. *Desire of Ages*, 815.

The Converted Peter

Then he received his commission. A work broader and more delicate than had heretofore been his was appointed him. Christ bade him feed the sheep and the lambs. In thus committing to his stewardship the souls for whom the Saviour had laid down his own life, Christ gave to Peter the strongest proof of confidence in his restoration. The once restless, boastful, self-confident disciple had become subdued and contrite. Henceforth he followed his Lord in self-denial and self-sacrifice. He was a partaker of Christ's sufferings; and when Christ shall sit upon the throne of His glory, Peter will be a partaker in His glory. *Christ's Object Lessons,* 154.

The first work that Christ entrusted to Peter on restoring him to the ministry was to feed the lambs. This was a work in which Peter had little experience. It would require great care and tenderness, much patience and perseverance. It called him to minister to those who were young in the faith, to teach the ignorant, to open the Scriptures to them, and to educate them for usefulness in Christ's service. Heretofore Peter had not been fitted to do this, or even to understand its importance. But this was the work which Jesus now called upon him to do. For this work his own experience of suffering and repentance had prepared him.

Before his fall, Peter was always speaking unadvisedly, from the impulse of the moment. He was always ready to correct others, and to express his mind, before he had a clear comprehension of himself or of what he had to say. But the converted Peter was very different. He retained his former fervor, but the grace of Christ regulated his zeal. He was no longer impetuous, self-confident, and self-exalted, but calm, self-possessed, and teachable. He could then feed the lambs as well as the sheep of Christ's flock.

The Saviour's manner of dealing with Peter had a lesson for him and for his brethren. It taught them to meet the transgressor with patience, sympathy, and forgiving love. Although Peter had denied his Lord, the love which Jesus bore him never faltered. Just such love should the undershepherd feel for the sheep and lambs committed to his care. Remembering his own weakness and failure, Peter was to deal with his flock as tenderly as Christ had dealt with him. *Desire of Ages*, 812-815.

Peter was now humble enough to understand the words of Christ, and without further questioning, the once restless, boastful, self-confident disciple became subdued and contrite. He followed his Lord indeed--the Lord he had denied. The thought that Christ had not denied and rejected him was to Peter a light and comfort and blessing. He felt that he could be crucified from choice, but it must be with his head downward. And he who was so close a partaker of Christ's sufferings will also be a partaker of His glory when He shall "sit upon the throne of his glory". *SDA Bible Commentary,* Volume 5, 1152.

On the day following the healing of the cripple, Annas and Caiaphas, with the other dignitaries of the temple, met together for the trial, and the prisoners were brought before them. In that very room and before some of those very men, Peter had shamefully denied his Lord. This came distinctly to his mind as he appeared for his own trial. He now had an opportunity of redeeming his cowardice.

Those present who remembered the part that Peter had acted at the trial of his Master, flattered themselves that he could now be intimidated by the threat of imprisonment and death. But the Peter who denied Christ in the hour of His greatest need was impulsive and self-confident, differing widely from the Peter who was brought before the Sanhedrin for examination. Since his fall he had been converted. He was no longer proud and boastful, but modest and self-distrustful. He was filled with the Holy Spirit, and by the help of this power he was resolved to remove the stain of his apostasy by honoring the name he had once disowned.

Hitherto the priests had avoided mentioning the crucifixion or the resurrection of Jesus. But now, in fulfillment of their purpose, they were forced to inquire of the accused how the cure of the impotent man had been accomplished. "By what power, or by what name, have ye done this?" they asked.

With holy boldness and in the power of the Spirit Peter fearlessly declared: "Be it known unto you all, and to all the people of Israel, that by the name of Jesus Christ of Nazareth, whom ye crucified, whom God raised from the dead, even by Him doth this man stand here before you whole. This is the stone which was set at nought of you builders, which is become the head of the corner. Neither is there salvation in any other: for there is none other name under heaven given among men, whereby we must be saved."

This courageous defense appalled the Jewish leaders. They had supposed that the disciples would be overcome with fear and confusion when brought before the Sanhedrin. But, instead, these witnesses spoke as Christ had spoken, with a convincing power that silenced their adversaries. There was no trace of fear in Peter's voice as he declared of Christ, "This is the stone which was set at nought of you builders, which is become the head of the corner." *Acts of the Apostles*, 62-63.

There was no trace of fear in Peter's voice as he declared of Christ, "This is the stone which was set at nought of you builders, which is become the head of the corner."

Then Peter, filled with the Holy Ghost, addressed the priests and elders respectfully, and declared: "Be it known unto you all, and to all the people of Israel, that by the name of Jesus Christ of Nazareth, whom ye crucified, whom God raised from the dead, even by Him doth this man stand here before you whole. This is the stone which was set at nought of you builders, which is become the head of the corner. Neither is there salvation in any other: for there is none other name under heaven given among men, whereby we must be saved."

The seal of Christ was on the words of Peter, and his countenance was illuminated by the Holy Spirit. Close beside him, as a convincing witness, stood the man who had been so miraculously cured. The appearance of this man, who but a few hours before was a helpless cripple, now restored to soundness of body, and being enlightened concerning Jesus of Nazareth, added a weight of testimony to the words of Peter. Priests, rulers, and people were silent. The rulers had no power to refute his statement. They had been obliged to hear that which they most desired not to hear: the fact of the resurrection of Jesus Christ, and His power in heaven to perform miracles through the medium of His apostles on earth.

The defense of Peter, in which he boldly avowed from whence his strength was obtained, appalled them. He had referred to the stone set at nought by the builders--meaning the authorities of the church, who should have perceived the value of Him whom they rejected--but which had nevertheless become the head of the corner. In those words he directly referred to Christ, who was the foundation stone of the church. *Story of Redemption*, 251, 252.

No restoration can be complete unless it reaches to the very depth of the soul by the transforming power of the Holy Spirit. Under the Holy Spirit's influence, Peter stood before a congregation of thousands, and in holy boldness charged the wicked priests and rulers with the very sin of which he himself had been guilty. "Ye denied the Holy One and the Just," he said, "and desired a murderer to be granted unto you; and killed the Prince of life, whom God hath raised from the dead; whereof we are witnesses. . . . And now, brethren, I wot that through ignorance ye did it, as did also your rulers. But those things, which God before had showed by the mouth of all his prophets, that Christ should suffer, he hath so fulfilled." There was now no moral insensibility upon Peter. As Christ's witness, under the inspiration of the Spirit of God, he gave evidence of his divine restoration. *The Youth's Instructor*, December 22, 1898.

I presented the matter before the hearers that Jesus the Lord of life and glory was crucified to please the malice of the Jews because the principles He presented did not coincide with their own ideas and ambitious aims. He condemned all guile, all underhanded work of policy for supremacy, and every unholy practice. Pilate and Herod became friends in crucifying Christ. They pleased the Jews in making effective their enmity against One whom Pilate proclaimed innocent. I presented to them ... Peter, who denied Him in His humiliation in the judgment hall. A few hours before, he had with great firmness assured his Master he would go with Him to prison and to death; and notwithstanding Jesus' declaration that he would, ere the cock crew, deny Him thrice, he was so self-confident that he took not the words of Christ as verity and truth. How little he knew himself! How soon circumstances tested his allegiance to his Master! He denied Jesus in the very hour he should have watched with Him in fervent prayer. When in the judgment hall he was accused of being one of this Man's disciples, he denied; and the third time he was accused, he emphasized his denial with cursing and swearing.

Said Christ, "Ye shall receive power, after that he Holy Ghost is come upon you: and ye shall be witnesses unto Me." The look of grief and sadness which Jesus gave Peter was not a hopeless look; it broke the heart of Peter, who denied his Lord.

The look of grief and sadness which Jesus gave Peter was not a hopeless look; it broke the heart of Peter, who denied his Lord.

But Peter was converted, and then after the crucifixion and resurrection of Christ when before the rulers, he boldly declared for Jesus, and charged the rulers with these words: "But ye denied the Holy One and the Just, and desired a murderer to be granted unto you; and killed the Prince of life." There Peter shows himself entirely a different man after his conversion than the self-confident, boasting Peter prior to his conversion. I presented before them the voice of the world, the enemies of Christ, saying to Christ's messengers, "Ye should not teach in this name" and "bring this Man's blood upon us." Did this threatening succeed? did it make cowards of the witnesses of Christ? No; they proclaimed the message given them of God; and they were shut up in prison, and God sent His angel to release them. The angel of the Lord by night opened the prison doors and brought them forth, and said, "Go, stand and speak in the temple to the people all the words of this life." This voice from the heavenly angels was directly opposite to that voice from the authorities, and which should they obey? "Then Peter and the other apostles answered and said, We ought to obey God rather than men. The God of our fathers raised up Jesus, whom ye slew and hanged on a tree. Him hath God exalted with His right hand to be a Prince and a Saviour, for to give repentance to Israel, and forgiveness of sins. And we are His witnesses of these things; and so is also the Holy Ghost, whom God hath given to them that obey Him. … Well, this is a little part of the words the Lord gave me to speak to the people. *Testimonies to Ministers*, 268.

Chapter Four

Preacher and Evangelist

Peter at Pentecost

Evening drew on, and an unearthly stillness hung over Calvary. The crowd dispersed, and many returned to Jerusalem greatly changed in spirit from what they had been in the morning. Many of them had then collected at the crucifixion from curiosity, and not from hatred toward Christ. Still they accepted the fabricated reports of the priests concerning him, and looked upon him as a malefactor. At the execution they had imbibed the spirit of the leading Jews, and, under an unnatural excitement, had united with the mob in mocking and railing against him.

But when the earth was draped with blackness, and they stood accused by their own consciences, reason again resumed her sway, and they felt guilty of doing a great wrong. No jest nor mocking laughter was heard in the midst of that fearful gloom; and when it was lifted, they solemnly made their way to their homes, awestruck and conscience-smitten. They were convinced that the accusations of the priests were false, that Jesus was no pretender; and a few weeks later they were among the thousands who became thorough converts to Christ, when Peter preached upon the day of Pentecost, and the great mystery of the cross was explained with other mysteries in regard to Messiah. *The Spirit of Prophecy*, Volume 3, 169.

The priests and rulers were greatly enraged at this wonderful manifestation, but they dared not give way to their malice, for fear of exposing themselves to the violence of the people. They had put the Nazarene to death; but here were His servants, unlettered men of Galilee, telling in all the languages then spoken, the story of His life and ministry. The priests, determined to account for the miraculous power of the disciples in some natural way, declared that they were drunken from partaking largely of the new wine prepared for the feast. Some of the most ignorant of the people present seized upon this suggestion as the truth, but the more intelligent knew it to be false; and those who understood the different languages testified to the accuracy with which these languages were used by the disciples.

In answer to the accusation of the priests Peter showed that this demonstration was in direct fulfillment of the prophecy of Joel, wherein he foretold that such power would come upon men to fit them for a special work. "Ye men of Judea, and all ye that dwell at Jerusalem," he said, "be this known unto you, and hearken to my words: for these are not drunken, as ye suppose, seeing it is but the third hour of the day. But this is that which was spoken by the prophet Joel: And it shall come to pass in the last days, saith God, I will pour out of My Spirit upon all flesh: and your sons and your daughters shall prophesy, and your young men shall see visions, and your old men shall dream dreams: and on My servants and on My handmaidens I will pour out in those days of My Spirit; and they shall prophesy."

With clearness and power Peter bore witness of the death and resurrection of Christ: "Ye men of Israel, hear these words: Jesus of Nazareth, a man approved of God among you by miracles and wonders and signs, which God did by Him in the midst of you, as ye yourselves also know: Him . . . ye have taken, and by wicked hands have crucified and slain: whom God hath raised up, having loosed the pains of death: because it was not possible that He should be holden of it."

Peter did not refer to the teachings of Christ to prove his position, because he knew that the prejudice of his hearers was so great that his words on this subject would be of no effect. Instead, he spoke to them of David, who was regarded by the Jews as one of the patriarchs of their nation. "David speaketh concerning Him," he declared: "I foresaw the Lord always before My face, for He is on My right hand, that I should not be moved: therefore did My heart rejoice, and My tongue was glad; moreover also My flesh shall rest in hope: because Thou wilt not leave My soul in hell, neither wilt Thou suffer Thine Holy One to see corruption. . . .

"Men and brethren, let me freely speak unto you of the patriarch David, that he is both dead and buried, and his sepulcher is with us unto this day." "He . . . spake of the resurrection of Christ, that His soul was not left in hell, neither His flesh did see corruption. This Jesus hath God raised up, whereof we all are witnesses." *Acts of the Apostles*, 40-42.

The arguments of the apostles alone, although clear and convincing, would not have removed the prejudice of the Jews which had withstood so much evidence. But the Holy Ghost sent those arguments home with divine power to their hearts. They were as sharp arrows of the Almighty, convicting them of their terrible guilt in rejecting and crucifying the Lord of glory. "Now when they heard this, they were pricked in their heart, and said unto Peter and to the rest of the apostles, Men and brethren, what shall we do? Then Peter said unto them, Repent, and be baptized every one of you in the name of Jesus Christ for the remission of sins, and ye shall receive the gift of the Holy Ghost."

The disciples and apostles of Christ had a deep sense of their own inefficiency, and with humiliation and prayer they joined their weakness to his strength, their ignorance to his wisdom, their unworthiness to his righteousness, their poverty to his inexhaustible wealth. Thus strengthened and equipped they hesitated not in the service of their Master. *The Spirit of Prophecy*, Volume 3, 273-274.

"Then Peter said unto them, Repent, and be baptized every one of you in the name of Jesus Christ for the remission of sins, and ye shall receive the gift of the Holy Ghost. For the promise is unto you, and to your children, and to all that are afar off, even as many as the Lord our God shall call."

Peter urged home upon the convicted people the fact that they had rejected Christ because they had been deceived by priests and rulers; and that if they continued to look to these men for counsel, and waited for them to acknowledge Christ before they dared to do so, they would never accept Him.

Peter urged home upon the convicted people the fact that they had rejected Christ because they had been deceived by priests and rulers; and that if they continued to look to these men for counsel, and waited for them to acknowledge Christ before they dared to do so, they would never accept Him. These powerful men, though making a profession of godliness, were ambitious for earthly riches and glory. They were not willing to come to Christ to receive light. *Acts of the Apostles*, 43.

In the work that was accomplished on the day of Pentecost, we may see what can be done by the exercise of faith. Those who believed in Christ were sealed by the Holy Spirit. As the disciples were assembled together, "there came a sound. . . as of a rushing mighty wind, and it filled all the house where they were sitting. And there appeared unto them cloven tongues like as of fire, and it sat upon each of them." And Peter stood up among them and spoke with mighty power. Among those who listened to him were devout Jews, who were sincere in their belief. But the power that accompanied the words of the speaker convinced them that Christ was indeed the Messiah. What a mighty work was accomplished! Three thousand were converted in one day. *SDA Bible Commentary,* Volume 6, 1055.

After the wonderful manifestation of the Holy Spirit on the Day of Pentecost, Peter exhorted the people to repentance and baptism in the name of Christ, for the remission of their sins; and he said: "Ye shall receive the gift of the Holy Ghost. For the promise is unto you, and to your children, and to all that are afar off, even as many as the Lord our God shall call." Acts 2:38, 39. *The Great Controversy,* ix.

At the Temple Gate

A short time after the descent of the Holy Spirit, and immediately after a season of earnest prayer, Peter and John, going up to the temple to worship, saw at the gate Beautiful a cripple, forty years of age, whose life, from his birth, had been one of pain and infirmity. This unfortunate man had long desired to see Jesus, that he might be healed; but he was almost helpless, and was far removed from the scene of the great Physician's labors. His pleadings at last induced some friends to bear him to the gate of the temple, but upon arriving there, he found that the One upon whom his hopes were centered, had been put to a cruel death.

His disappointment excited the sympathy of those who knew for how long he had eagerly hoped to be healed by Jesus, and daily they brought him to the temple, in order that passers-by might be induced by pity to give him a trifle to relieve his wants. As Peter and John passed, he asked an alms from them. The disciples regarded him compassionately, and Peter said, "Look on us. And he gave heed unto them, expecting to receive something of them. Then Peter said, Silver and gold have I none." As Peter thus declared his poverty, the countenance of the cripple fell; but it grew bright with hope as the apostle continued, "But such as I have give I thee: In the name of Jesus Christ of Nazareth rise up and walk.

"And he took him by the right hand, and lifted him up: and immediately his feet and ankle-bones received strength. And he leaping up stood, and walked, and entered with them into the temple, walking, and leaping, and praising God. And all the people saw him walking and praising God: and they knew that it was he which sat for alms at the Beautiful Gate of the temple: and they were filled with wonder and amazement at that which had happened."

"And as the lame man which was healed held Peter and John, all the people ran together unto them in the porch that is called Solomon's, greatly wondering." They were astonished that the disciples could perform miracles similar to those performed by Jesus. Yet here was this man, for forty years a helpless cripple, now rejoicing in the full use of his limbs, free from pain, and happy in believing in Jesus.

When the disciples saw the amazement of the people, Peter asked, "Why marvel ye at this? or why look ye so earnestly on us, as though by our own power or holiness we had made this man to walk?" He assured them that the cure had been wrought in the name and through the merits of Jesus of Nazareth, whom God had raised from the dead. "His name through faith in His name," the apostle declared, "hath made this man strong, whom ye see and know: yea, the faith which is by Him hath given him this perfect soundness in the presence of you all."

The apostles spoke plainly of the great sin of the Jews in rejecting and putting to death the Prince of life; but they were careful not to drive their hearers to despair. "Ye denied the Holy One and the Just," Peter said, "and desired a murderer to be granted unto you; and killed the Prince of life, whom God hath raised from the dead; whereof we are witnesses." "And now, brethren, I wot that through ignorance ye did it, as did also your rulers. But those things, which God before had showed by the mouth of all His prophets, that Christ should suffer, He hath so fulfilled." He declared that the Holy Spirit was calling upon them to repent and be converted, and assured them that there was no hope of salvation except through the mercy of the One whom they had crucified. Only through faith in Him could their sins be forgiven. *Acts of the Apostles*, 57-59.

With mighty power the disciples preached a crucified and risen Saviour. Signs and wonders were wrought by them in the name of Jesus; the sick were healed; and a man who had been lame from his birth was restored to perfect soundness and entered with Peter and John into the temple, walking and leaping and praising God in the sight of all the people. The news spread, and the people began to press around the disciples. Many ran together, greatly astonished at the cure that had been wrought.

When Jesus died, the priests thought that no more miracles would be performed among them, that the excitement would die out and the people would again turn to the traditions of men. But lo! right among them the disciples were working miracles, and the people were filled with amazement. Jesus had been crucified, and they wondered where His followers had obtained this power. When He was alive, they thought that He imparted power to them; but when He died, they expected the miracles to cease. Peter understood their perplexity and said to them, "Ye men of Israel, why marvel ye at this? or why look ye so earnestly on us, as though by our own power or holiness we had made this man to walk? The God of Abraham, and of Isaac, and of Jacob, the God of our fathers, hath glorified His Son Jesus; whom ye delivered up, and denied Him in the presence of Pilate, when he was determined to let Him go. But ye denied the Holy One and the Just, and desired a murderer to be granted unto you; and killed the Prince of life, whom God hath raised from the dead; whereof we are witnesses. And His name through faith in His name hath made this man strong, whom ye see and know." *Early Writings,* 192.

We read in the Acts of the Apostles that after the miracle at the temple gate, many signs and wonders were wrought, and many were healed. "Then the high-priest rose up, . . . and all they that were with him, . . . and were filled with indignation." Why?--Because the great adversary of God and man was provoked that he could not hold his captives in torment, and that Christ was doing the very work that he had declared in Nazareth he would do. He had said, "The Spirit of the Lord is upon me, because he hath anointed me to preach the gospel to the poor; he hath sent me to heal the brokenhearted, to preach deliverance to the captives, and recovering of sight to the blind, to set at liberty them that are bruised, to preach the acceptable year of the Lord." *Review and Herald*, April 22, 1890.

On the day following the healing of the cripple, Annas and Caiaphas, with the other dignitaries of the temple, met together for the trial, and the prisoners were brought before them. In that very room and before some of those very men, Peter had shamefully denied his Lord. This came distinctly to his mind as he appeared for his own trial. He now had an opportunity of redeeming his cowardice.

Those present who remembered the part that Peter had acted at the trial of his Master, flattered themselves that he could now be intimidated by the threat of imprisonment and death. But the Peter who denied Christ in the hour of His greatest need was impulsive and self-confident, differing widely from the Peter who was brought before the Sanhedrin for examination. Since his fall he had been converted. He was no longer proud and boastful, but modest and self-distrustful. He was filled with the Holy Spirit, and by the help of this power he was resolved to remove the stain of his apostasy by honoring the name he had once disowned.

Hitherto the priests had avoided mentioning the crucifixion or the resurrection of Jesus. But now, in fulfillment of their purpose, they were forced to inquire of the accused how the cure of the impotent man had been accomplished. "By what power, or by what name, have ye done this?" they asked.

With holy boldness and in the power of the Spirit Peter fearlessly declared: "Be it known unto you all, and to all the people of Israel, that by the name of Jesus Christ of Nazareth, whom ye crucified, whom God raised from the dead, even by Him doth this man stand here before you whole. This is the stone which was set at nought of you builders, which is become the head of the corner. Neither is there salvation in any other: for there is none other name under heaven given among men, whereby we must be saved."

This courageous defense appalled the Jewish leaders. They had supposed that the disciples would be overcome with fear and confusion when brought before the Sanhedrin. But, instead, these witnesses spoke as Christ had spoken, with a convincing power that silenced their adversaries. There was no trace of fear in Peter's voice as he declared of Christ, "This is the stone which was set at nought of you builders, which is become the head of the corner."

Peter here used a figure of speech familiar to the priests. The prophets had spoken of the rejected stone; and Christ Himself, speaking on one occasion to the priests and elders, said: "Did ye never read in the Scriptures, The stone which the builders rejected, the same is become the head of the corner: this is the Lord's doing, and it is marvelous in our eyes? Therefore say I unto you, The kingdom of God shall be taken from you, and given to a nation bringing forth the fruits thereof. And whosoever shall fall on this stone shall be broken: but on whomsoever it shall fall, it will grind him to powder." Matthew 21:42-44.

As the priests listened to the apostles' fearless words, "they took knowledge of them, that they had been with Jesus." *Acts of the Apostles*, 62-64.

The authorities commanded them not to speak any more nor to teach in the name of Jesus. "But Peter and John answered and said unto them, Whether it be right in the sight of God to hearken unto you more than unto God, judge ye. For we cannot but speak the things we have seen and heard."

When the disciples preached Christ and him crucified, after his resurrection, the authorities commanded them not to speak any more nor to teach in the name of Jesus. "But Peter and John answered and said unto them, Whether it be right in the sight of God to hearken unto you more than unto God, judge ye. For we cannot but speak the things we have seen and heard." They continued to preach Jesus and him crucified, and afterward raised from the dead. The sick were healed, and thousands were added to the church. "Then the high priest rose up, and all that were with him (which is the sect of the Sadducees), and were filled with indignation, and laid their hands on the apostles, and put them in the common prison." *Review and Herald*, January 1, 1889.

There is a prospect before us of a continued struggle, at the risk of imprisonment, loss of property, and even of life itself, to defend the law of God, which is made void by the laws of men. In this situation worldly policy will urge an outward compliance with the laws of the land, for the sake of peace and harmony. And there are some who will even urge such a course from the Scripture: "Let every soul be subject unto the higher powers. . . . The powers that be are ordained of God."

But what has been the course of God's servants in ages past? When the disciples preached Christ and Him crucified, after His resurrection, the authorities commanded them not to speak any more nor to teach in the name of Jesus. "But Peter and John answered and said unto them, Whether it be right in the sight of God to hearken unto you more than unto God, judge ye. For we cannot but speak the things which we have seen and heard." They continued to preach the good news of salvation through Christ, and the power of God witnessed to the message. The sick were healed, and thousands were added to the church. "Then the high priest rose up, and all they that were with him, (which is the sect of the Sadducees,) and were filled with indignation, and laid their hands on the apostles, and put them in the common prison."

But the God of heaven, the mighty Ruler of the universe, took this matter into His own hands; for men were warring against His work. He showed them plainly that there is a ruler above man, whose authority must be respected. The Lord sent His angel by night to open the prison doors, and he brought forth these men whom God had commissioned to do His work. The rulers said, Speak not "at all nor teach in the name of Jesus;" but the heavenly messenger sent by God said, "Go, stand and speak in the temple to the people all the words of this life." *Testimonies for the Church*, Volume 5, 712, 713.

"We Ought to Obey God"

In the history of prophets and apostles, are many noble examples of loyalty to God. Christ's witnesses have endured imprisonment, torture, and death itself, rather than break God's commands. The record left by Peter and John is as heroic as any in the gospel dispensation. As they stood for the second time before the men who seemed bent on their destruction, no fear or hesitation could be discerned in their words or attitude. And when the high priest said, "Did we not straitly command you that ye should not teach in this name? and, behold, ye have filled Jerusalem with your doctrine, and intend to bring this Man's blood upon us," Peter answered, "We ought to obey God rather than men." It was an angel from heaven who delivered them from prison and bade them teach in the temple. In following his directions they were obeying the divine command, and this they must continue to do at whatever cost to themselves. *Acts of the Apostles*, 81.

Peter, with the other apostles, took up the same line of defense he had followed at his former trial: "Then Peter and the other apostles answered and said, We ought to obey God rather than men." It was the angel sent by God who delivered them from prison, and who commanded them to teach in the temple. In following his directions they were obeying the divine command, which they must continue to do at any cost to themselves. Peter continued: "The God of our fathers raised up Jesus, whom ye slew and hanged on a tree. Him hath God exalted with his right hand to be a Prince and a Saviour, for to give repentance to Israel, and forgiveness of sins. And we are his witnesses of these things; and so is also the Holy Ghost, whom God hath given to them that obey him." *The Spirit of Prophecy*, Volume 3, 289.

And then they shut the disciples up in a prison, that the message of God should no longer be given to the people, but the angel of the Lord was there. All heaven was looking upon them then, and the angels are now looking upon those who are living at this closing period of earth's history. The angel of the Lord came by night to the servants of God, and said, "Go, stand and speak in the temple to the people all the words of this life." Here was an order directly contrary to the command given by the potentates of the earth. But the direction of the angel was from the highest court in the universe. Did the apostles say to the angel, "We cannot do this until we have consulted the magistrates, and received permission of them?"--No; God had said "Go," and they went forth to speak according to his commandment. In the morning their enemies called a council, and sent to the prison that they might be brought before them, but when the officers found them not, they said, "The prison truly found we shut with all safety, . . . but when we had opened, we found no man within." The angel of God could take them through the prison walls, and they had no power to hold them. We have the same God today, and he works on the same plan. When they said the prison was shut, the chief priest doubted the keeper. God was working and the enemy was working, and the battle was waged between the God of heaven and the powers that be. Then the captain sent the officers and had them brought, because they feared the people, and when they were before the council, the high-priest asked, "Did not we straitly command you, that ye should not teach in his name? and, behold, ye have filled Jerusalem with your doctrine." Then the apostles answered, "We ought to obey God rather than men." We ought to be obedient to all the laws of our country, except when those laws come in collision with the law of God, and then we must obey God, irrespective of everything else. *Review and Herald*, April 22, 1890.

The influence of the world did not prevail with Peter. He was converted, and after the resurrection of Christ, he was endowed with the Holy Spirit, and then with boldness charged the rulers with their guilt in putting Christ to death. He said, "Ye denied the Holy One and the Just, and desired a murderer to be granted unto you; and killed the Prince of life." After his conversion, Peter showed that he was an entirely changed man. He was not the self-confident, boasting Peter that he had been before his conversion. And when the enemies of Christ threatened him, and charged him that he should not teach any more in the name of Jesus, and bring this man's blood upon them, their threatening did not intimidate the servant of Christ. He did not turn coward, but with the other apostles proclaimed the name of Christ until they were all shut up in prison. But the angel of the Lord by night opened the prison doors, and brought them forth, and said, "Go, stand and speak in the temple to the people all the words of this life." The command of the angel was opposed to the command of the authorities, and which should they obey? "Then Peter and the other apostles answered and said, We ought to obey God rather than men." *Review and Herald*, February 26, 1895.

The influence of the world did not prevail with Peter. He was converted, and after the resurrection of Christ, he was endowed with the Holy Spirit, and then with boldness charged the rulers with their guilt in putting Christ to death.

Christ declared of the Jews, "In vain they do worship me, teaching for doctrines the commandments of men." This is being done today. The commandments of men are exalted, and men are trying to force their fellow-men to render obedience to them. But in no case are we to take the word of men before the Word of God. "We ought to obey God rather than men," declared Peter. And Christ in his Sermon on the Mount spoke clearly and distinctly regarding the importance of God's commandments. "Think not," he said, "that I am come to destroy the law, or the prophets; I am not come to destroy, but to fulfil. For verily I say unto you, Till heaven and earth pass, one jot or one tittle shall in nowise pass from the law, till all be fulfilled. Whosoever therefore shall break one of these least commandments, and shall teach men so, he shall be called the least in the kingdom of heaven; but whosoever shall do and teach them, the same shall be called great in the kingdom of heaven."

But God never compels men to obey him. Together truth and error take the field. The light shines forth amid moral darkness, and men are left to choose their own leader. *Signs of the Times*, May 13, 1897.

Paul writes to the Romans, "If it be possible, as much as lieth in you, live peaceably with all men." But there is a point beyond which it is impossible to maintain union and harmony without the sacrifice of principle. Separation then becomes an absolute duty. The laws of nations should be respected when they do not conflict with the laws of God. But when there is collision between them, every true disciple of Christ will say, as did the apostle Peter when commanded to speak no more in the name of Jesus, "We ought to obey God rather than men." *Signs of the Times*, November 8, 1899.

Paul writes to the Romans, "If it be possible, as much as lieth in you, live peaceably with all men." But there is a point beyond which it is impossible to maintain union and harmony without the sacrifice of principle. Separation then becomes an absolute duty.

Chapter Five
Peter the Apostle

Peter Discerns Ananias and Sapphira's Designs

"But a certain man named Ananias, with Sapphira his wife, sold a possession, and kept back part of the price, his wife also being privy to it, and brought a certain part, and laid it at the apostles' feet." This couple had noted the fact that those who had parted with their possessions to supply the wants of their poorer brethren were held in high esteem among the believers. They therefore, upon consulting together, decided to sell their property, and affect to give all the proceeds into the general fund, but really to retain a large share for themselves. They thus designed to receive their living, which they intended to estimate much higher than it really was, from the common stock, and to secure the high esteem of their brethren.

But a holy God hates hypocrisy and falsehood. The apostles were impressed by a sense of the true state of the case, and when

Ananias presented himself with his offering, representing it as the entire proceeds of the sale of his property, Peter said to him, "Ananias, why hath Satan filled thine heart to lie to the Holy Ghost, and to keep back part of the price of the land? While it remained, was it not thine own? and after it was sold, was it not in thine own power? Why hast thou conceived this thing in thine heart? Thou hast not lied unto men, but unto God. And Ananias, hearing these words, fell down, and gave up the ghost; and great fear came on all them that heard these things."

Peter asked, "Was it not thine own?" thus showing that no undue influence had been brought to bear upon Ananias and Sapphira to compel them to sacrifice their possessions to the general good. They had acted from choice. But in pretending to be wrought upon by the Holy Ghost, and attempting to deceive the apostles, they had lied to the Almighty.

"And it was about the space of three hours after, when his wife, not knowing what was done, came in. And Peter answered unto her, Tell me whether ye sold the land for so much? And she said, Yea, for so much. Then Peter said unto her, How is it that ye have agreed together to tempt the Spirit of the Lord? Behold, the feet of them which have buried thy husband are at the door, and shall carry thee out. Then fell she down straightway at his feet, and yielded up the ghost; and the young men came in, and found her dead, and, carrying her forth, buried her by her husband. And great fear came upon all the church, and upon as many as heard these things."

This signal manifestation of the wrath of God upon the dissemblers was a check which Infinite Wisdom knew was needed. The church would have been disgraced; if, in the rapid increase of professed Christians, there were persons professing to serve God, but worshiping mammon. There are many Ananiases and Sapphiras in our day, whom Satan tempts to dissemble, because of their love of money. By various plans and excuses they withhold from the treasury of God the means intrusted to them for the advancement of the cause of God. Should the punishment of Ananias and Sapphira be visited upon this class, there would be many dead bodies in our churches requiring burial.

This marked judgment upon two avaricious hypocrites, whose sin had been detected by the evidence of the Spirit of God to the apostles, excited the reverential awe of all the new converts. From that time there was greater caution manifested by them, and a more thorough self-examination, testing the motives of their actions. In any great religious movement there is always a class who are carried away by the current of feeling, but who soon reveal selfishness and vain-glory. Such persons can never be an honor to the cause they advocate.

The discernment of the apostles in detecting hidden sin added to the confidence of their brethren in them and the message which they preached. *Redemption: Or the Miracles of Christ, the Mighty One,* (1877), 21-23.

Peter Rebukes the Sorcerer

Among the converts in Samaria was one Simon, who, by the power of Satan through sorcerers, had gained great fame among the people. "To whom they all gave heed, from the least to the greatest, saying, This man is the great power of God. And to him they had regard, because that of long time he had bewitched them with sorceries." But when he saw a greater power manifested by the apostles in healing the sick and in converting souls to the truth, he thought that by uniting with the believers in Christ he might do wonders equal to those accomplished by the apostles. He hoped thus to add greatly to his fame and wealth, for he made merchandise of his sorceries and Satanic arts, pretending to impart their secrets to others.

His darkened mind could not distinguish between the power of the Holy Ghost and that of Satan. He went to Peter and offered him money if he would give him power to heal the sick, and impart to men the Holy Ghost, by laying his hands upon them. Peter was filled with horror at such a proposal, and severely rebuked the presumption of Simon. Said he, "Thy money perish with thee, because thou hast thought that the gift of God may be purchased with money. Thou hast neither part nor lot in this matter; for thy heart is not right in the sight of God. Repent therefore of this thy wickedness, and pray God, if perhaps the thought of thine heart may be forgiven thee. For I perceive that thou art in the gall of bitterness, and in the bond of iniquity."

The magician trembled with fear as his sin was presented before him in this vivid manner. He began to perceive his own wicked audacity, and entreated Peter to pray that the wrath of God might not come upon him for his presumptuous sin. Peter had, with startling force, shown Simon that he was yet untouched by the grace of God; for if his mind had been thus enlightened, he would have known that the sacred power of the Holy Spirit could not be bought or sold for money. Christ, at the infinite price of himself, had obtained for his people the power of the Holy Spirit, to be given only to his chosen instruments, whose lives must be free from selfishness and sin. *The Spirit of Prophecy*, Volume 3, 302, 303.

Peter had, with startling force, shown Simon that he was yet untouched by the grace of God; for if his mind had been thus enlightened, he would have known that the sacred power of the Holy Spirit could not be bought or sold for money.

Peter Heals Aeneas

In the course of his ministry the apostle Peter visited the believers at Lydda. Here he healed Aeneas, who for eight years had been confined to his bed with palsy. "Aeneas, Jesus Christ maketh thee whole," the apostle said; "arise, and make thy bed." "He arose immediately. And all that dwelt at Lydda and Saron saw him, and turned to the Lord." *Acts of the Apostles*, 131.

Dorcas Raised

Joppa was near Lydda, and at that time Tabitha-- called Dorcas by interpretation--lay there dead. She had been a worthy disciple of Jesus Christ, and her life had been characterized by deeds of charity and kindness to the poor and sorrowful, and by zeal in the cause of truth. Her death was a great loss; the infant church could not well spare her noble efforts. When the believers heard of the marvelous cures which Peter had performed in Lydda, they greatly desired him to come to Joppa. Messengers were sent to him to solicit his presence there.

"Then Peter arose and went with them. When he was come, they brought him into the upper chamber; and all the widows stood by him weeping, and showing the coats and garments which Dorcas made while she was with them." Peter had the weeping and wailing friends sent from the room. He then kneeled down, and prayed fervently to God to restore life and health to the pulseless body of Dorcas; "and turning him to the body said, Tabitha, arise. And she opened her eyes; and when she saw Peter, she sat up. And he gave her his hand, and lifted her up; and when he had called the saints and widows, he presented her alive." This great work of raising the dead to life was the means of converting many in Joppa to the faith of Jesus. *The Spirit of Prophecy,* Volume 3, 323-324.

At Joppa, which was near Lydda, there lived a woman named Dorcas, whose good deeds had made her greatly beloved. She was a worthy disciple of Jesus, and her life was filled with acts of kindness. She knew who needed comfortable clothing and who needed sympathy, and she freely ministered to the poor and the sorrowful. Her skillful fingers were more active than her tongue.

"And it came to pass in those days, that she was sick, and died." The church in Joppa realized their loss, and hearing that Peter was at Lydda, the believers sent messengers to him, "desiring him that he would not delay to come to them. Then Peter arose and went with them. When he was come, they brought him into the upper chamber: and all the widows stood by him weeping, and showing the coats and garments which Dorcas made, while she was with them." In view of the life of service that Dorcas had lived, it is little wonder that they mourned, that warm teardrops fell upon the inanimate clay.

The apostle's heart was touched with sympathy as he beheld their sorrow. Then, directing that the weeping friends be sent from the room, he kneeled down and prayed fervently to God to restore Dorcas to life and health. Turning to the body, he said, "Tabitha, arise. And she opened her eyes: and when she saw Peter, she sat up." Dorcas had been of great service to the church, and God saw fit to bring her back from the land of the enemy, that her skill and energy might still be a blessing to others, and also that by this manifestation of His power the cause of Christ might be strengthened. *Acts of the Apostles*, 131-132.

The Shadow of Peter

In Jerusalem, where the deepest prejudice existed, and where the most confused ideas prevailed in regard to Him who had been crucified as a malefactor, the disciples continued to speak with boldness the words of life, setting before the Jews the work and mission of Christ, His crucifixion, resurrection, and ascension. Priests and rulers heard with amazement the clear, bold testimony of the apostles. The power of the risen Saviour had indeed fallen on the disciples, and their work was accompanied by signs and miracles that daily increased the number of believers. Along the streets where the disciples were to pass, the people laid their sick "on beds and couches, that at the least the shadow of Peter passing by might overshadow some of them." Here also were brought those vexed with unclean spirits. The crowds gathered round them, and those who were healed shouted the praises of God and glorified the name of the Redeemer. *Acts of the Apostles*, 77.

The Lord continued to bless his followers as they bore their testimony. Believers were added to the church, the sick were healed, and wonderful works were wrought, "insomuch that they brought forth the sick into the streets, and laid them on beds and couches, that at the least the shadow of Peter passing by might overshadow some of them. There came also a multitude out of the cities round about unto Jerusalem, bringing sick folks, and them which were vexed with unclean spirits: and they were healed every one."

Here were light and evidence that none could gainsay. But did these signs have weight with the priests and rulers?--No; they were filled with indignation, and laid their hands on the apostles, and put them in the common prison. Satan was striving to make of none effect the work of Christ, to blot his name from the earth. But Heaven was determined to give evidence to the people that Jesus was the Son of God. An angel of the Lord was commissioned to go to the prison, and say to the disciples, "Go, stand and speak in the temple to the people all the words of this life." *The Youth's Instructor*, October 11, 1900.

Chapter Six

The Gospel to the Gentiles

Peter's Rooftop Vision

It was while Peter was still at Joppa that he was called by God to take the gospel to Cornelius, in Caesarea. *Acts of the Apostles*, 132.

While Cornelius was praying, there came to him a heavenly messenger, who addressed him by name. The centurion was afraid, yet he knew that the angel had been sent by God, and he said, "What is it, Lord?" "Thy prayers and thine alms are come up for a memorial before God," the angel answered. "Send men to Joppa, and call for one Simon, whose surname is Peter: he lodgeth with one Simon a tanner, whose house is by the seaside."

The explicitness of these directions, in which was named even the occupation of the man with whom Peter was staying, shows that heaven is acquainted with the history and business of men in every station in life. God is familiar with the experience and work of the humble laborer as well as with that of the king upon his throne. *Review and Herald*, April 6, 1911.

The angel, after his interview with Cornelius, went to Peter, in Joppa. At the time, Peter was praying upon the housetop of his lodging, and we read that he "became very hungry, and would have eaten: but while they made ready, he fell into a trance." It was not for physical food alone that Peter hungered. As from the housetop he viewed the city of Joppa and the surrounding country he hungered for the salvation of his countrymen. He had an intense desire to point out to them from the Scriptures the prophecies relating to the sufferings and death of Christ.

In the vision Peter "saw heaven opened, and a certain vessel descending unto him, as it had been a great sheet knit at the four corners, and let down to the earth: wherein were all manner of four-footed beasts of the earth, and wild beasts, and creeping things, and fowls of the air. And there came a voice to him, Rise, Peter; kill, and eat. But Peter said, Not so, Lord; for I have never eaten anything that is common or unclean. And the voice spake unto him again the second time, What God hath cleansed, that call not thou common. This was done thrice: and the vessel was received up again into heaven."

This vision conveyed to Peter both reproof and instruction. It revealed to him the purpose of God—that by the death of Christ the Gentiles should be made fellow heirs with the Jews to the blessings of salvation.

This vision conveyed to Peter both reproof and instruction. It revealed to him the purpose of God—that by the death of Christ the Gentiles should be made fellow heirs with the Jews to the blessings of salvation. As yet none of the disciples had preached the gospel to the Gentiles. In their minds the middle wall of partition, broken down by the death of Christ, still existed, and their labors had been confined to the Jews, for they had looked upon the Gentiles as excluded from the blessings of the gospel. Now the Lord was seeking to teach Peter the world-wide extent of the divine plan. *Acts of the Apostles,* 135.

Here we may perceive the workings of God's plan to set the machinery in motion, whereby his will may be done on earth as it is done in Heaven. Peter had not yet preached the gospel to the Gentiles. Many of them had been interested listeners to the truths which he taught; but the middle wall of partition, which the death of Christ had broken down, still existed in the minds of the apostles, and excluded the Gentiles from the privileges of the gospel. The Greek Jews had received the labors of the apostles, and many of them had responded to those efforts by embracing the faith of Jesus; but the conversion of Cornelius was to be the first one of importance among the Gentiles. *The Spirit of Prophecy*, Volume 3, 327.

The time had come for an entirely new phase of work to be entered upon by the church of Christ. The door that many of the Jewish converts had closed against the Gentiles was now to be thrown open. And the Gentiles who accepted the gospel were to be regarded as on an equality with the Jewish disciples, without the necessity of observing the rite of circumcision.

How carefully the Lord worked to overcome the prejudice against the Gentiles that had been so firmly fixed in Peter's mind by his Jewish training! By the vision of the sheet and its contents He sought to divest the apostle's mind of this prejudice and to teach the important truth that in heaven there is no respect of persons; that Jew and Gentile are alike precious in God's sight; that through Christ the heathen may be made partakers of the blessings and privileges of the gospel.

While Peter was meditating on the meaning of the vision, the men sent from Cornelius arrived in Joppa and stood before the gate of his lodginghouse. Then the Spirit said to him, "Behold, three men seek thee. Arise therefore, and get thee down, and go with them, doubting nothing: for I have sent them."

To Peter this was a trying command, and it was with reluctance at every step that he undertook the duty laid upon him; but he dared not disobey. He "went down to the men which were sent unto him from Cornelius; and said, Behold, I am he whom ye seek: what is the cause wherefore ye are come?" They told him of their singular errand, saying, "Cornelius the centurion, a just man, and one that feareth God, and of good report among all the nation of the Jews, was warned from God by a holy angel to send for thee into his house, and to hear words of thee."

In obedience to the directions just received from God, the apostle promised to go with them. On the following morning he set out for Caesarea, accompanied by six of his brethren. These were to be witnesses of all that he should say or do while visiting the Gentiles, for Peter knew that he would be called to account for so direct a violation of the Jewish teachings.

As Peter entered the house of the Gentile, Cornelius did not salute him as an ordinary visitor, but as one honored of Heaven and sent to him by God. It is an Eastern custom to bow before a prince or other high dignitary and for children to bow before their parents; but Cornelius, overwhelmed with reverence for the one sent by God to teach him, fell at the apostle's feet and worshiped him. Peter was horror-stricken, and he lifted the centurion up, saying, "Stand up; I myself also am a man."

While the messengers of Cornelius had been gone upon their errand, the centurion "had called together his kinsmen and near friends," that they as well as he might hear the preaching of the gospel. When Peter arrived, he found a large company eagerly waiting to listen to his words.

To those assembled, Peter spoke first of the custom of the Jews, saying that it was looked upon as unlawful for Jews to mingle socially with the Gentiles, that to do this involved ceremonial defilement. "Ye know," he said, "how that it is an unlawful thing for a man that is a Jew to keep company, or come unto one of another nation; but God hath showed me that I should not call any man common or unclean. Therefore came I unto you without gainsaying, as soon as I was sent for: I ask therefore for what intent ye have sent for me?"

Cornelius then related his experience and the words of the angel, saying in conclusion, "Immediately therefore I sent to thee; and thou hast well done that thou art come. Now therefore are we all here present before God, to hear all things that are commanded thee of God."

Peter said, "Of a truth I perceive that God is no respecter of persons: but in every nation he that feareth Him, and worketh righteousness, is accepted with Him."

Then to that company of attentive hearers the apostle preached Christ--His life, His miracles, His betrayal and crucifixion, His resurrection and ascension, and His work in heaven as man's representative and advocate. As Peter pointed those present to Jesus as the sinner's only hope, he himself understood more fully the meaning of the vision he had seen, and his heart glowed with the spirit of the truth that he was presenting.

Suddenly the discourse was interrupted by the descent of the Holy Spirit. "While Peter yet spake these words, the Holy Ghost fell on all them which heard the word. And they of the circumcision which believed were astonished, as many as came with Peter, because that on the Gentiles also was poured out the gift of the Holy Ghost. For they heard them speak with tongues, and magnify God.

"Then answered Peter, Can any man forbid water, that these should not be baptized, which have received the Holy Ghost as well as we? And he commanded them to be baptized in the name of the Lord."

Thus was the gospel brought to those who had been strangers and foreigners, making them fellow citizens with the saints, and members of the household of God. The conversion of Cornelius and his household was but the first fruits of a harvest to be gathered in. From this household a wide-spread work of grace was carried on in that heathen city. *Acts of the Apostles*, 136-139.

The vision of all manner of live beasts, which the sheet contained, and of which Peter was commanded to kill and eat, being assured that what God had cleansed should not be called common or unclean by him, was simply an illustration presenting to his mind the true position of the Gentiles; that by the death of Christ they were made fellow-heirs with the Israel of God.

The vision of all manner of live beasts, which the sheet contained, and of which Peter was commanded to kill and eat, being assured that what God had cleansed should not be called common or unclean by him, was simply an illustration presenting to his mind the true position of the Gentiles; that by the death of Christ they were made fellow-heirs with the Israel of God. It conveyed to Peter both reproof and instruction. His labors had heretofore been confined entirely to the Jews; and he had looked upon the Gentiles as an unclean race, and excluded from the promises of God. His mind was now being led to comprehend the world-wide extent of the plan of God.

Even while he pondered over the vision, it was explained to him. "Now while Peter doubted in himself what this vision which he had seen should mean, behold, the men which were sent from Cornelius had made inquiry for Simon's house, and stood before the gate, and called, and asked whether Simon, which was surnamed Peter, were lodged there. While Peter thought on the vision, the Spirit said unto him, Behold, three men seek thee. Arise therefore, and get thee down, and go with them, doubting nothing; for I have sent them." *The Spirit of Prophecy*, Volume 3, 328.

The Christian Council at Jerusalem

The questions thus brought under the consideration of the council seemed to present insurmountable difficulties, viewed in whatever light. But the Holy Ghost had, in reality, already settled this problem, upon the decision of which depended the prosperity, and even the existence, of the Christian church. Grace, wisdom, and sanctified judgment were given to the apostles to decide the vexed question.

Peter reasoned that the Holy Ghost had decided the matter by descending with equal power upon the uncircumcised Gentiles and the circumcised Jews. He recounted his vision, in which God had presented before him a sheet filled with all manner of four-footed beasts, and had bidden him kill and eat; that when he had refused, affirming that he had never eaten that which was common or unclean, God had said, "What God hath cleansed, that call not thou common."

He related the plain interpretation of these words, which was given to him almost immediately in his summons to go to the Gentile centurion, and instruct him in the faith of Christ. This message showed that God was not respecter of persons, but accepted and acknowledged those who feared him, and worked righteousness. Peter told of his astonishment, when, in speaking the words of truth to the Gentiles, he witnessed the Holy Spirit take possession of his hearers, both Jews and Gentiles. The same light and glory that was reflected upon the circumcised Jews, shone also upon the countenances of the uncircumcised Gentiles. This was the warning of God that he should not regard the one as inferior to the other; for the blood of Jesus Christ could cleanse from all uncleanness.

Peter had reasoned once before, in like manner, with his brethren, concerning the conversion of Cornelius and his friends, and his fellowship with them. On that occasion he had related how the Holy Ghost fell on them, and had said, "Forasmuch then as God gave them the like gift as he did unto us, who believed on the Lord Jesus Christ, what was I that I could resist God?" Now, with equal fervor and force, he said, "God, which knoweth the hearts, bare them witness, giving them the Holy Ghost, even as he did unto us, and put no difference between us and them, purifying their hearts by faith. Now, therefore, why tempt ye God, to put a yoke upon the neck of the disciples, which neither our fathers nor we were able to bear?"

This yoke was not the law of the ten commandments, as those who oppose the binding claim of the law assert; but Peter referred to the law of ceremonies, which was made null and void by the crucifixion of Christ. This address of Peter brought the assembly to a point where they could listen with reason to Paul and Barnabas, who related their experience in working among the Gentiles. "Then all the multitude kept silence, and gave audience to Barnabas and Paul, declaring what miracles and wonders God had wrought among the Gentiles by them." *The Spirit of Prophecy*, Volume 3, 372-374.

Paul Reproves Peter

Even the best of men, if left to themselves, will make grave blunders. The more responsibilities placed upon the human agent, the higher his position to dictate and control, the more mischief he is sure to do in perverting minds and hearts if he does not carefully follow the way of the Lord. At Antioch Peter failed in the principles of integrity. Paul had to withstand his subverting influence face to face. This is recorded that others may profit by it, and that the lesson may be a solemn warning to the men in high places, that they may not fail in integrity, but keep close to principle.

At Antioch Peter failed in the principles of integrity. Paul had to withstand his subverting influence face to face.

After all the failures of Peter, after his fall and restoration, his long course of service, his intimate acquaintance with Christ, his knowledge of Christ's pure, straightforward practice of principle; after all the instruction he had received, all the gifts and knowledge and great influence in preaching and teaching the Word, is it not strange that he should dissemble and evade the principles of the gospel, for fear of man, or in order to gain his esteem? Is it not strange that he should waver, and be two-sided in his position? May God give every man a sense of his own personal helplessness to steer his own vessel straight and safely into the harbor. The grace of Christ is essential every day. His matchless grace alone can save our feet from falling. *SDA Bible Commentary,* Volume 6, 1108.

When Peter, at a later date, visited Antioch, he won the confidence of many by his prudent conduct toward the Gentile converts. For a time he acted in accordance with the light given from heaven. He so far overcame his natural prejudice as to sit at table with the Gentile converts. But when certain Jews who were zealous for the ceremonial law, came from Jerusalem, Peter injudiciously changed his deportment toward the converts from paganism. A number of the Jews "dissembled likewise with him; insomuch that Barnabas also was carried away with their dissimulation." This revelation of weakness on the part of those who had been respected and loved as leaders, left a most painful impression on the minds of the Gentile believers. The church was threatened with division. But Paul, who saw the subverting influence of the wrong done to the church through the double part acted by Peter, openly rebuked him for thus disguising his true sentiments. In the presence of the church, Paul inquired of Peter, "If thou, being a Jew, livest after the manner of Gentiles, and not as do the Jews, why compellest thou the Gentiles to live as do the Jews?" Galatians 2:13, 14.

Peter saw the error into which he had fallen, and immediately set about repairing the evil that had been wrought, so far as was in his power. God, who knows the end from the beginning, permitted Peter to reveal this weakness of character in order that the tried apostle might see that there was nothing in himself whereof he might boast. Even the best of men, if left to themselves, will err in judgment. God also saw that in time to come some would be so deluded as to claim for Peter and his pretended successors the exalted prerogatives that belong to God alone. And this record of the apostle's weakness was to remain as a proof of his fallibility and of the fact that he stood in no way above the level of the other apostles. *Acts of the Apostles*, 197-199.

Chapter Seven

Arrest and Escape

Peter in Prison

Herod was professedly a proselyte to the Jewish faith, and apparently very zealous in perpetuating the ceremonies of the law. The government of Judea was in his hands, subject to Claudius, the Roman emperor; he also held the position of tetrarch of Galilee. Herod was anxious to obtain the favor of the Jews, hoping thus to make secure his offices and honors. He therefore proceeded to carry out the desires of the Jews in persecuting the church of Christ. He began his work by spoiling the houses and goods of the believers; he then began to imprison the leading ones. He seized upon James and cast him into prison, and there sent an executioner to kill him with a sword, as another Herod had caused the prophet John to be beheaded. He then became bolder, seeing that the Jews were well pleased with his acts, and imprisoned Peter.

These cruelties were performed during the sacred occasion of the passover.

James was one of the three favored disciples who had been brought into the closest relationship with Christ. James, John, and Peter were his chief witnesses after his death. They saw the transfiguration of the Saviour, and beheld him glorified. They were in the garden with him during the night of his agony. James and John were the sons of Zebedee, the ones whom Jesus had asked, "Are ye able to drink of the cup that I shall drink of, and to be baptized with the baptism that I am baptized with?" When James was rudely thrust into prison, and unceremoniously summoned to execution, he understood more fully than ever before, the words of his Lord upon that occasion.

There was great grief and consternation at the death of James. When Peter was also imprisoned, the entire church engaged in fasting and prayer. While the Jews were celebrating the memorial of their deliverance from Egypt, and pretending great zeal for the law, they were at the same time persecuting and murdering the believers in Christ, thus transgressing every principle of that law. At these great religious gatherings they stirred one another up against the Christians, till they were united in a bitter hatred of them. *The Spirit of Prophecy*, Volume 3, 334, 335.

Herod's act in putting James to death was applauded by the Jews, though some complained of the private manner in which it was accomplished, maintaining that a public execution would have more thoroughly intimidated the believers and those sympathizing with them. Herod therefore held Peter in custody, meaning still further to gratify the Jews by the public spectacle of his death. But it was suggested that it would not be safe to bring the veteran apostle out for execution before all the people then assembled in Jerusalem. It was feared that the sight of him being led out to die might excite the pity of the multitude.

The priests and elders also feared lest Peter might make one of those powerful appeals which had frequently aroused the people to study the life and character of Jesus--appeals which they, with all their arguments, had been unable to controvert. Peter's zeal in advocating the cause of Christ had led many to take their stand for the gospel, and the rulers feared that should he be given an opportunity to defend his faith in the presence of the multitude who had come to the city to worship, his release would be demanded at the hands of the king.

While, upon various pretexts, the execution of Peter was being delayed until after the Passover, the members of the church had time for deep searching of heart and earnest prayer. They prayed without ceasing for Peter, for they felt that he could not be spared from the cause. They realized that they had reached a place where, without the special help of God, the church of Christ would be destroyed.

Meanwhile worshipers from every nation sought the temple which had been dedicated to the worship of God. Glittering with gold and precious stones, it was a vision of beauty and grandeur. But Jehovah was no longer to be found in that palace of loveliness. Israel as a nation had divorced herself from God. When Christ, near the close of His earthly ministry, looked for the last time upon the interior of the temple, He said, "Behold, your house is left unto you desolate." Matthew 23:38. Hitherto He had called the temple His Father's house; but as the Son of God passed out from those walls, God's presence was withdrawn forever from the temple built to His glory.

The day of Peter's execution was at last appointed, but still the prayers of the believers ascended to heaven; and while all their energies and sympathies were called out in fervent appeals for help, angels of God were watching over the imprisoned apostle.

Remembering the former escape of the apostles from prison, Herod on this occasion had taken double precautions. To prevent all possibility of release, Peter had been put under the charge of sixteen soldiers, who, in different watches, guarded him day and night. In his cell he was placed between two soldiers and was bound by two chains, each chain being fastened to the wrist of one of the soldiers. He was unable to move without their knowledge. With the prison doors securely fastened, and a strong guard before them, all chance of rescue or escape through human means was cut off. But man's extremity is God's opportunity.

Peter was confined in a rock-hewn cell, the doors of which were strongly bolted and barred; and the soldiers on guard were made answerable for the safekeeping of the prisoner. But the bolts and bars and the Roman guard, which effectually cut off all possibility of human aid, were but to make more complete the triumph of God in the deliverance of Peter. Herod was lifting his hand against Omnipotence, and he was to be utterly defeated. By the putting forth of His might, God was about to save the precious life that the Jews were plotting to destroy.

Peter was confined in a rock-hewn cell, the doors of which were strongly bolted and barred; and the soldiers on guard were made answerable for the safekeeping of the prisoner. But the bolts and bars and the Roman guard, which effectually cut off all possibility of human aid, were but to make more complete the triumph of God in the deliverance of Peter.

It is the last night before the proposed execution. A mighty angel is sent from heaven to rescue Peter. The strong gates that shut in the saint of God open without the aid of human hands. The angel of the Most High passes through, and the gates close noiselessly behind him. He enters the cell, and there lies Peter, sleeping the peaceful sleep of perfect trust.

The light that surrounds the angel fills the cell, but does not rouse the apostle. Not until he feels the touch of the angel's hand and hears a voice saying, "Arise up quickly," does he awaken sufficiently to see his cell illuminated by the light of heaven, and an angel of great glory standing before him. Mechanically he obeys the word spoken to him, and as in rising he lifts his hands he is dimly conscious that the chains have fallen from his wrists.

Again the voice of the heavenly messenger bids him, "Gird thyself, and bind on thy sandals," and again Peter mechanically obeys, keeping his wondering gaze riveted upon his visitor and believing himself to be dreaming or in a vision. Once more the angel commands, "Cast thy garment about thee, and follow me." He moves toward the door, followed by the usually talkative Peter, now dumb from amazement. They step over the guard and reach the heavily bolted door, which of its own accord swings open and closes again immediately, while the guards within and without are motionless at their post.

The second door, also guarded within and without, is reached. It opens as did the first, with no creaking of hinges or rattling of iron bolts. They pass through, and it closes again as noiselessly. In the same way they pass through the third gateway and find themselves in the open street. No word is spoken; there is no sound of footsteps. The angel glides on in front, encircled by a light of dazzling brightness, and Peter, bewildered, and still believing himself to be in a dream, follows his deliverer. Thus they pass on through one street, and then, the mission of the angel being accomplished, he suddenly disappears.

The heavenly light faded away, and Peter felt himself to be in profound darkness; but as his eyes became accustomed to the darkness, it gradually seemed to lessen, and he found himself alone in the silent street, with the cool night air blowing upon his brow. He now realized that he was free, in a familiar part of the city; he recognized the place as one that he had often frequented and had expected to pass on the morrow for the last time. *Acts of the Apostles*, 144-148.

There are many passages of Scripture which skeptical critics have declared to be uninspired, but which, in their tender adaptation to the needs of men, are God's own messages of comfort to His trusting children. A beautiful illustration of this occurs in the history of the apostle Peter. Peter was in prison, expecting to be brought forth next day to death; he was sleeping at night "between two soldiers, bound with two chains: and the keepers before the door kept the prison. And, behold, the angel of the Lord came upon him, and a light shined in the prison: and he smote Peter on the side, and raised him up, saying, Arise up quickly. And his chains fell off from his hands." Peter, suddenly awaking, was amazed at the brightness that flooded his dungeon, and the celestial beauty of the heavenly messenger. He understood not the scene, but he knew that he was free, and in his bewilderment and joy he would have gone forth from the prison unprotected from the cold night air. The angel of God, noting all the circumstances, said, with tender care for the apostle's need: "Gird thyself, and bind on thy sandals." Peter mechanically obeyed; but so entranced was he with the revelation of the glory of heaven that he did not think to take his cloak. Then the angel bade him: "Cast thy garment about thee, and follow me. And he went out, and followed him; and wist not that it was true which was done by the angel; but thought he saw a vision. When they were past the first and the second ward, they came unto the iron gate that leadeth unto the city; which opened to them of his own accord: and they went out, and passed on through one street; and forthwith the angel departed from him." The apostle found himself in the streets of Jerusalem alone. "And when Peter was come to himself, he said, Now I know of a surety,"--it was not a dream or a vision, but an actual occurrence,--"that the Lord hath sent His angel, and hath delivered me out of the hand of Herod, and from all the expectation of the people of the Jews." *Testimonies for the Church*, Volume 5, 748.

He tried to recall the events of the last few moments. He remembered falling asleep, bound between the two soldiers, with his sandals and outer garment removed. He examined his person, and found himself fully dressed, and girded.

His wrists, swollen from wearing the cruel irons, were now free from the manacles, and he realized that his freedom was no delusion, but a blessed reality. On the morrow he was to have been led forth to die; but lo, an angel had delivered him from prison and from death. "And when Peter was come to himself, he said, Now I know of a surety that the Lord hath sent his angel, and hath delivered me out of the hand of Herod, and from all the expectation of the people of the Jews."

The apostle made his way direct to the house where his brethren were assembled together for prayer; he found them engaged in earnest prayer for him at that moment. "And as Peter knocked at the door of the gate, a damsel came to hearken, named Rhoda. And when she knew Peter's voice, she opened not the gate for gladness, but ran in, and told how Peter stood before the gate. And they said unto her, Thou art mad. But she constantly affirmed that it was even so. Then said they, It is his angel. But Peter continued knocking; and when they had opened the door, and saw him, they were astonished. But he, beckoning unto them with the hand to hold their peace, declared unto them how the Lord had brought him out of the prison. And he said, Go show these things unto James, and to the brethren. And he departed, and went into another place."

Joy and praise filled the hearts of the fasting, praying believers, that God had heard and answered their prayers, and delivered Peter from the hand of Herod. In the morning the people gathered together to witness the execution of the apostle. Herod sent officers to bring Peter from prison with great display of arms and guard, in order to insure against his escape, to intimidate all sympathizers, and to exhibit his own power. *The Spirit of Prophecy*, Volume 3, 340, 341.

When the keepers before the door found that Peter had escaped, they were seized with terror. It had been expressly stated that their lives would be required for the life of their charge, and because of this they had been especially vigilant. When the officers came for Peter, the soldiers were still at the door of the prison, the bolts and bars were still fast, the chains were still secured to the wrists of the two soldiers; but the prisoner was gone.

When the report of Peter's escape was brought to Herod, he was exasperated and enraged. Charging the prison guard with unfaithfulness, he ordered them to be put to death. Herod knew that no human power had rescued Peter, but he was determined not to acknowledge that a divine power had frustrated his design, and he set himself in bold defiance against God. *Acts of the* Apostles, 149.

Only the sense of God's presence can banish the fear that, for the timid child, would make life a burden. Let him fix in his memory the promise, "The angel of the Lord encampeth round about them that fear him, and delivereth them." Psalm 34:7. Let him read that wonderful story of Elisha in the mountain city, and, between him and the hosts of armed foemen, a mighty encircling band of heavenly angels. Let him read how to Peter, in prison and condemned to death, God's angel appeared; how, past the armed guards, the massive doors and great iron gateway with their bolts and bars, the angel led God's servant forth in safety. *Child Guidance*, 43.

Chapter Eight

Peter's Legacy and Writings

Peter's Influence on Youth

The lessons taught to children and youth make an impression upon their minds which influences their characters in a far greater degree than older persons imagine. In my childhood a minister who came to my father's house at Poland, Maine, read the chapter in Acts in regard to the deliverance of Peter, when an angel of God took the prey from the enemy who had determined to destroy him. The chapter was read slowly and solemnly, and it made an impression on my young mind that has kept the narrative vividly before me to this day. *Evangelism*, 580.

Many a youth has been flattered that he has ability as a natural gift; when the ability he thinks he has, can be attained only through diligent training and culture, learning the meekness and lowliness of Christ. Believing he is naturally gifted, he thinks there is no necessity of putting his mind to the task of mastering his lessons; and before he is aware, he is fast in the snare of Satan. God permits him to be attacked by the enemy, in order that he may understand his own weakness. He is permitted to make some decided blunder, and is plunged into painful humiliation. But when he is writhing under a sense of his own weakness, he is not to be judged harshly. This is the time above all others when he needs a judicious counselor, a true friend, who has discernment of character. This is the time when he needs a friend who is led by the Spirit of God, and who will deal patiently and faithfully with the erring, and lift up the soul that is bowed down. He is not to be lifted up by the aid of flattery. No one is authorized to deal out to the soul this delusive intoxicant of Satan. Rather he is to be pointed to the first rounds of the ladder, and his stumbling feet are to be placed on the lowest round of the ladder of progress. Peter says, "Add to your faith virtue; and to virtue knowledge; and to knowledge temperance; and to temperance patience; and to patience godliness; and to godliness brotherly kindness; and to brotherly kindness charity. For if these things be in you, and abound, they make you that ye shall neither be barren nor unfruitful in the knowledge of our Lord Jesus Christ."

Let the erring one be encouraged to climb step by step, round by round. The effort may be painful to him, but it will be by far the best lesson he has ever learned; for by so doing he will become acquainted with his own weakness, and thus be enabled to avoid in the future the errors of the past. *Fundamentals of Christian Education*, 304, 305.

The charge given to Peter by Christ just before his ascension was, "Feed my lambs," "feed my sheep;" and this commission has been given to every minister and worker. But the work has been neglected. While something has been done for the education and religious training of the youth, there is still a great lack. Many more need to be encouraged and helped. There is not that personal labor given which the case requires. It is not the ministers alone who have neglected this solemn work of saving the youth; the members of the churches will have to settle with the Master for their indifference and neglect of duty. *Review and Herald*, January 10, 1899.

The great Shepherd has under-shepherds, to whom He delegates the care of His sheep and lambs. The first work that Christ entrusted to Peter, on restoring him to the ministry, was to feed the lambs. [See John 21:15.] This was a work in which Peter had had little experience. It would require great care and tenderness, much patience and perseverance. It called him to minister to the children and youth, and to those young in the faith, to teach the ignorant, to open the Scriptures to them, and to educate them for usefulness in Christ's service. Heretofore Peter had not been fitted to do this, or even to understand its importance.

The first work that Christ entrusted to Peter, on restoring him to the ministry, was to feed the lambs. [See John 21:15.]… It called him to minister to the children and youth, and to those young in the faith, to teach the ignorant, to open the Scriptures to them, and to educate them for usefulness in Christ's service.

The question that Christ put to Peter was significant. He mentioned only one condition of discipleship and service. "Lovest thou Me?" He said. This is the essential qualification. Though Peter might possess every other, without the love of Christ he could not be a faithful shepherd over the Lord's flock. Knowledge, benevolence, eloquence, gratitude, and zeal are all aids in the good work; but without the love of Jesus in the heart, the work of the Christian minister will prove a failure.

The lesson which Christ taught him by the Sea of Galilee, Peter carried with him throughout his life. Writing by the Holy Spirit to the churches, he said:

"The elders which are among you I exhort, who am also an elder, and a witness of the sufferings of Christ, and also a partaker of the glory that shall be revealed: Feed the flock of God which is among you, taking the oversight thereof, not by constraint, but willingly; not for filthy lucre, but of a ready mind; neither as being lords over God's heritage, but being ensamples to the flock. And when the Chief Shepherd shall appear, ye shall receive a crown of glory that fadeth not away." [1 Peter 5:1-4.] *Gospel Workers*, 182, 183.

Throughout his ministry, Peter faithfully watched over the flock entrusted to his care, and thus proved himself worthy of the charge and responsibility given him by the Saviour. Ever he exalted Jesus of Nazareth as the Hope of Israel, the Saviour of mankind. He brought his own life under the discipline of the Master Worker. By every means within his power he sought to educate the believers for active service. His godly example and untiring activity inspired many young men of promise to give themselves wholly to the work of the ministry. As time went on, the apostle's influence as an educator and leader increased; and while he never lost his burden to labor especially for the Jews, yet he bore his testimony in many lands and strengthened the faith of multitudes in the gospel. *Acts of the Apostles*, 516.

If the youth could only awake to deeply feel their need of strength from God to resist the temptations of Satan, precious victories would be theirs, and they would obtain a valuable experience in the Christian warfare. How few of the young think of the exhortation of the inspired apostle Peter: "Be sober, be vigilant; because your adversary the devil, as a roaring lion, walketh about, seeking whom he may devour: whom resist steadfast in the faith." In the vision given to John he saw the power of Satan over men and exclaimed: "Woe to the inhabiters of the earth and of the sea! for the devil is come down unto you, having great wrath, because he knoweth that he hath but a short time." *Testimonies for the Church*, Volume 3, 373.

With the apostle Peter, I would say; "I will not be negligent to put you always in remembrance of these things, though ye know them, and be established in the present truth." And with the apostle, dear youth, I would lift my voice in earnest exhortation to you to "give diligence to make your calling and election sure: for if ye do these things, ye shall never fall: for so an entrance shall be ministered unto you abundantly into the everlasting kingdom of our Lord and Saviour Jesus Christ." *The Canadian Union Messenger*, September 3, 1907.

Peter's Inspired Epistles

In Isaiah's prophecy, Christ is declared to be both a sure foundation and a stone of stumbling. The apostle Peter, writing by inspiration of the Holy Spirit, clearly shows to whom Christ is a foundation stone, and to whom a rock of offense:

"If so be ye have tasted that the Lord is gracious. To whom coming, as unto a living stone, disallowed indeed of men, but chosen of God, and precious, ye also, as lively stones, are built up a spiritual house, an holy priesthood, to offer up spiritual sacrifices, acceptable to God by Jesus Christ. Wherefore also it is contained in the Scripture, Behold, I lay in Sion a chief cornerstone, elect, precious: and he that believeth on Him shall not be confounded. Unto you therefore which believe He is precious: but unto them which be disobedient, the stone which the builders disallowed, the same is made the head of the corner, and a stone of stumbling, and a rock of offense, even to them which stumble at the word, being disobedient." 1 Peter 2:3-8. *Desire of Ages*, 599.

In the later years of his ministry, Peter was inspired to write to the believers "scattered throughout Pontus, Galatia, Cappadocia, Asia, and Bithynia." His letters were the means of reviving the courage and strengthening the faith of those who were enduring trial and affliction, and of renewing to good works those who through manifold temptations were in danger of losing their hold upon God. These letters bear the impress of having been written by one in whom the sufferings of Christ and also His consolation had been made to abound; one whose entire being had been transformed by grace, and whose hope of eternal life was sure and steadfast. . . .

The apostle's words were written for the instruction of believers in every age, and they have a special significance for those who live at the time when "the end of all things is at hand." His exhortations and warnings, and his words of faith and courage, are needed by every soul who would maintain his faith "steadfast unto the end." Hebrews 3:14. *Acts of the Apostles*, 517, 518.

Centuries before the Saviour's advent Moses had pointed to the Rock of Israel's salvation. The psalmist had sung of "the Rock of my strength." Isaiah had written, "Thus saith the Lord God, Behold, I lay in Zion for a foundation a stone, a tried stone, a precious cornerstone, a sure foundation." Deuteronomy 32:4; Psalm 62:7; Isaiah 28:16. Peter himself, writing by inspiration, applies this prophecy to Jesus. He says, "If ye have tasted that the Lord is gracious: unto whom coming, a living stone, rejected indeed of men, but with God elect, precious, ye also, as living stones, are built up a spiritual house." 1 Peter 2:3-5, R. V. *Desire of Ages*, 413.

Looking forward with prophetic vision to the perilous times into which the church of Christ was to enter, the apostle exhorted the believers to steadfastness in the face of trial and suffering. "Beloved," he wrote, "think it not strange concerning the fiery trial which is to try you."

Trial is part of the education given in the school of Christ, to purify God's children from the dross of earthliness. It is because God is leading His children that trying experiences come to them. Trials and obstacles are His chosen methods of discipline, and His appointed conditions of success. He who reads the hearts of men knows their weaknesses better than they themselves can know them. He sees that some have qualifications which, if rightly directed, could be used in the advancement of His work. In His providence He brings these souls into different positions and varied circumstances, that they may discover the defects that are concealed from their own knowledge. He gives them opportunity to overcome these defects and to fit themselves for service. Often He permits the fires of affliction to burn, that they may be purified. *Acts of the Apostles*, 524.

Under the inspiration of the Spirit, the apostle Peter represents Christians as those who have purified their souls in obeying the truth.

Under the inspiration of the Spirit, the apostle Peter represents Christians as those who have purified their souls in obeying the truth. Just in accordance with the faith and love we bring into our work will be the power brought into it. No man can create faith. The Spirit operating upon and enlightening the human mind, creates faith in God. In the Scriptures faith is stated to be the gift of God, powerful unto salvation, enlightening the hearts of those who search for truth as for hidden treasure. The Spirit of God impresses the truth on the heart. The gospel is called the power of God unto salvation because God alone can make the truth a power which sanctifies the soul. He alone can render the cross of Christ triumphant (MS 56, 1899). *SDA Bible Commentary*, Volume 7, 940.

Writing by the inspiration of the Spirit of God, the apostle Peter says: "Whom having not seen, ye love; in whom, though now ye see Him not, yet believing, ye rejoice with joy unspeakable and full of glory; receiving the end of your faith, even the salvation of your souls. Of which salvation the prophets have inquired and searched diligently, who prophesied of the grace that should come unto you; searching what, or what manner of time the Spirit of Christ which was in them did signify, when it testified beforehand the sufferings of Christ, and the glory that should follow. Unto whom it was revealed, that not unto themselves, but unto us they did minister the things, which are now reported unto you by them that have preached the Gospel unto you with the Holy Ghost sent down from heaven; which things the angels desire to look into." *Signs of the Times*, July 12, 1899.

Peter and Apostles Subject to Mistakes

The disciples themselves yet cherished a regard for the ceremonial law, and were too willing to make concessions, hoping by so doing to gain the confidence of their countrymen, remove their prejudice, and win them to faith in Christ as the world's Redeemer. Paul's great object in visiting Jerusalem was to conciliate the church of Palestine. So long as they continued to cherish prejudice against him, they were constantly working to counteract his influence. He felt that if he could by any lawful concession on his part win them to the truth, he would remove a very great obstacle to the success of the gospel in other places. But he was not authorized of God to concede so much as they had asked. This concession was not in harmony with his teachings, nor with the firm integrity of his character. His advisers were not infallible. Though some of these men wrote under the inspiration of the Spirit of God, yet when not under its direct influence they sometimes erred. It will be remembered that on one occasion Paul withstood Peter to the face because he was acting a double part. *Sketches from the Life of Paul*, 213.

Peter's Ladder

It is the work of the youth to make advancement day by day. Peter says, "Add to your faith virtue; and to virtue knowledge; and to knowledge temperance; and to temperance patience; and to patience godliness; and to godliness brotherly kindness; and to brotherly kindness charity. For if these things be in you, and abound, they make you that ye shall neither be barren nor unfruitful in the knowledge of our Lord Jesus Christ."

All these successive steps are not to be kept before the mind's eye, and counted as you start; but fixing the eye upon Jesus, with an eye single to the glory of God, you will make advancement. You cannot reach the full measure of the stature of Christ in a day, and you would sink in despair could you behold all the difficulties that must be met and overcome. You have Satan to contend with, and he will seek by every possible device to attract your mind from Christ. *Messages to Young People*, 45.

The body is not kept under by many professed Sabbathkeepers. Some have embraced the Sabbath whose minds have ever been depraved. And when they embraced the truth they did not feel the necessity of turning square about and changing their whole course of action. They have been for years following the inclinations of an unregenerate heart, and have been swayed by the corrupt passions of their carnal natures, which had defaced the image of God in them and defiled everything they touched; therefore their entire future life would be all too short, at the longest, to climb Peter's ladder of Christian perfection, preparatory to their entering into the kingdom of God. But there are not many who feel that they cannot be saved by a profession of the truth, unless they become sanctified through the truth in answer to the prayer of our divine Lord to His Father: "Sanctify them through Thy truth: Thy word is truth." *Testimonies for the Church*, Volume 2, 479.

Many teachers permit their minds to take too narrow and low a range. They do not keep the divine plan ever in view, but are fixing their eyes upon worldly models. Look up, "where Christ sitteth on the right hand of God," and then labor that your pupils may be conformed to His perfect character. Point the youth to Peter's ladder of eight rounds, and place their feet, not on the highest round, but on the lowest, and with earnest solicitation urge them to climb to the very top.

Christ, who connects earth with heaven, is the ladder. The base is planted firmly on the earth in His humanity; the topmost round reaches to the throne of God in His divinity. The humanity of Christ embraces fallen humanity, while His divinity lays hold upon the throne of God. We are saved by climbing round after round of the ladder, looking to Christ, clinging to Christ, mounting step by step to the height of Christ, so that He is made unto us wisdom and righteousness and sanctification and redemption. Faith, virtue, knowledge, temperance, patience, godliness, brotherly kindness, and charity are the rounds of this ladder. All these graces are to be manifested in the Christian character; and "if ye do these things, ye shall never fall: for so an entrance shall be ministered unto you abundantly into the everlasting kingdom of our Lord and Saviour Jesus Christ." 2 Peter 1:10, 11. *Testimonies for the Church*, Volume 6, 147.

These words are full of instruction, and strike the keynote of victory. The apostle presents before the believers the ladder of Christian progress, every step of which represents advancement in the knowledge of God, and in the climbing of which there is to be no standstill. Faith, virtue, knowledge, temperance, patience, godliness, brotherly kindness, and charity are the rounds of the ladder. We are saved by climbing round after round, mounting step after step, to the height of Christ's ideal for us. Thus He is made unto us wisdom, and righteousness, and sanctification, and redemption.

God has called His people to glory and virtue, and these will be manifest in the lives of all who are truly connected with Him. Having become partakers of the heavenly gift, they are to go on unto perfection, being "kept by the power of God through faith." 1 Peter 1:5. It is the glory of God to give His virtue to His children. He desires to see men and women reaching the highest standard; and when by faith they lay hold of the power of Christ, when they plead His unfailing promises, and claim them as their own, when with an importunity that will not be denied they seek for the power of the Holy Spirit, they will be made complete in Him. *Acts of the Apostles*, 530.

I have before spoken to you of the plan of addition--Peter's ladder of eight rounds. "Add to your faith virtue, and to virtue, knowledge; and to knowledge, temperance; and to temperance, patience; and to patience, godliness; and to godliness, brotherly kindness; and to brotherly kindness, charity. For if these things be in you, and abound, they make you that ye shall neither be barren nor unfruitful in the knowledge of our Lord Jesus Christ." *Review and Herald*, January 4, 1887.

A new and symmetrical character may be formed by laying up one grace and good deed upon another, thus climbing Peter's ladder of eight rounds in sanctification. A character thus built will be harmonious in all its paths. Faith will sustain works, for faith works by love and purifies the soul. *Signs of the Times*, May 6, 1880.

A new and symmetrical character may be formed by laying up one grace and good deed upon another, thus climbing Peter's ladder of eight rounds in sanctification. A character thus built will be harmonious in all its paths.

We have men claiming sanctification. Their works will show if they are transformed into the image of Christ. Sanctification is not brought about instantaneously, but it is accomplished by climbing the rounds of Peter's ladder of eight rounds. We must step on the first in order to reach the highest. This ladder reaches from earth to heaven, and every soul that enters the city of God will have to climb this ladder of self-denial, and this can be accomplished by laying hold of the merits of a crucified and risen Saviour. Without this strength, temptation will sweep us down the current to final destruction. *Manuscript Releases*, Volume 3, 84.

Lessons from Peter's Trials

I would that we all could continually bear in mind what Christ is to us, and what we are to him. If we could constantly realize this relation between Christ and our souls, we would rejoice in hope of the glory of God, even in the midst of tribulation. But when tribulation comes upon us, how hard it seems to rejoice; for we are like Peter, and look upon the troublous waves about us instead of keeping the eye fixed upon Jesus. But I would have you see the importance of keeping the eye fixed upon him who is the Author and Finisher of our faith; for when we take our eyes off the difficulties and trials and fix them upon our Helper, we shall see his matchless charms, and know that "all things work together for good to them that love God." *Signs of the Times*, March 28, 1892.

Christ gave His life to reproach; He suffered, being tempted; He was falsely accused, and His motives were misjudged. But if men consider not the dear sacrifice made for them, if they are not willing to die to self and to the world, they become spiritually blind. They do not discern the value of eternal riches. They do not love or honor the Christ-life. They know not at what they stumble. They are enslaved by their own carnal inclinations, which they are not willing to relinquish. And when trials and difficulties arise, they give up building a temple for God, a pure, holy character after the divine similitude. Instead of driving them to the solid rock, the least rebuff makes cowards of them. Scorn and ridicule make them ashamed of Jesus, and they turn from Him to associate with and do honor to His persecutors. Thus, like Peter in the judgment-hall, they put Christ to open shame. Such can not endure all things for Christ's sake. They can not endure to the end. They have not counted the cost. They have not been converted to Christ. *Signs of the Times*, July 28, 1898.

It was necessary for Peter to learn his own defects of character, and his need of the power and grace of Christ. The Lord could not save him from trial, but He could have saved him from defeat. Had Peter been willing to receive Christ's warning, he would have been watching unto prayer. He would have walked with fear and trembling lest his feet should stumble. And he would have received divine help so that Satan could not have gained the victory.

It was through self-sufficiency that Peter fell; and it was through repentance and humiliation that his feet were again established. In the record of his experience every repenting sinner may find encouragement. Though Peter had grievously sinned, he was not forsaken. The words of Christ were written upon his soul, "I have prayed for thee, that thy faith fail not." Luke 22:32. In his bitter agony of remorse, this prayer, and the memory of Christ's look of love and pity, gave him hope. Christ after His resurrection remembered Peter, and gave the angel the message for the women, "Go your way, tell His disciples and Peter that He goeth before you into Galilee; there shall ye see Him." Mark 16:7. Peter's repentance was accepted by the sin-pardoning Saviour.

And the same compassion that reached out to rescue Peter is extended to every soul who has fallen under temptation. It is Satan's special device to lead man into sin, and then leave him, helpless and trembling, fearing to seek for pardon. But why should we fear, when God has said, "Let him take hold of My strength, that he may make peace with Me; and he shall make peace with Me?" Isaiah 27:5. Every provision has been made for our infirmities, every encouragement offered us to come to Christ. *Christ's Object Lessons*, 155, 156.

How little did Peter understand his own weakness. He could not discern but that his spirit was all right, even when he sought to make of none effect the solemn words of Christ which opened to them a future full of sorrow and of suffering, both to him and to them. Christ saw that unless Peter was changed in spirit, he would not be able to endure the test and the trial of his Lord's rejection, humiliation, condemnation, and death. To his Master's warning words he responded, "Lord, I am ready to go with thee, both into prison, and to death. And he said, I tell thee, Peter, the cock shall not crow this day, before thou shalt thrice deny that thou knowest me."

We see how human nature can be deceived, how human nature can be misled, because Satan is allowed to step in between the human soul and Jesus. The word of Christ needs to be spoken with authority, "Get thee behind me, Satan." Let me come close to my servant, that he may not be overcome, that he may believe my words rather than the words of men; for what I speak is truth and righteousness. *Manuscript Releases*, Volume 7, 202.

Thus Peter wrote to the believers at a time of peculiar trial to the church. Many had already become partakers of Christ's sufferings, and soon the church was to undergo a period of terrible persecution. Within a few brief years many of those who had stood as teachers and leaders in the church were to lay down their lives for the gospel. Soon grievous wolves were to enter in, not sparing the flock. But none of these things were to bring discouragement to those whose hopes were centered in Christ. With words of encouragement and good cheer Peter directed the minds of the believers from present trials and future scenes of suffering "to an inheritance incorruptible, and undefiled, and that fadeth not away." "The God of all grace," he fervently prayed, "who hath called us unto His eternal glory by Christ Jesus, after that ye have suffered awhile, make you perfect, stablish, strengthen, settle you. To Him be glory and dominion for ever and ever. Amen." *Acts of the Apostles*, 528.

Peter had severe trials to pass through, but although he was called to go to prison and to death for Christ's sake, never again did he waver from his allegiance.

In the answers that Peter gave to the Lord's thrice-repeated question, a different spirit is manifested from what we find in the boastful assurances before the crucifixion of Christ. Peter was a converted man, and showed in his life that transforming grace had taken possession of his heart. As firm as a rock, he ever after stood boldly up to witness for Christ. Jesus had said to Peter, "Simon, behold, Satan hath desired to have you, that he may sift you as wheat: but I have prayed for thee, that thy faith fail not; and when thou art converted, strengthen thy brethren." Peter had severe trials to pass through, but although he was called to go to prison and to death for Christ's sake, never again did he waver from his allegiance. *Review and Herald*, April 7, 1891.

In this hope of a sure inheritance in the earth made new the early Christians rejoiced, even in times of severe trial and affliction. "Ye greatly rejoice," Peter wrote, "though now for a season, if need be, ye are in heaviness through manifold temptations: that the trial of your faith, being much more precious than of gold that perisheth, though it be tried with fire, might be found unto praise and honor and glory at the appearing of Jesus Christ: whom having not seen, ye love; in whom, though now ye see Him not, . . . ye rejoice with joy unspeakable and full of glory: receiving the end of your faith, even the salvation of your souls."

The apostle's words were written for the instruction of believers in every age, and they have a special significance for those who live at the time when "the end of all things is at hand." His exhortations and warnings, and his words of faith and courage, are needed by every soul who would maintain his faith "steadfast unto the end." Hebrews 3:14. *Acts of the Apostles*, 517, 518.

The apostle exhorted the believers to study the Scriptures, through a proper understanding of which they might make sure work for eternity. Peter realized that in the experience of every soul who is finally victorious there would be scenes of perplexity and trial; but he knew also that an understanding of the Scriptures would enable the tempted one to bring to mind promises that would comfort the heart and strengthen faith in the Mighty One. *Acts of the Apostles*, 521.

There had been a time in Peter's experience when he was unwilling to see the cross in the work of Christ. When the Saviour made known to the disciples His impending sufferings and death, Peter exclaimed, "Be it far from Thee, Lord: this shall not be unto Thee." Matthew 16:22. Self-pity, which shrank from fellowship with Christ in suffering, prompted Peter's remonstrance. It was to the disciple a bitter lesson, and one which he learned but slowly, that the path of Christ on earth lay through agony and humiliation. But in the heat of the furnace fire he was to learn its lesson. Now, when his once active form was bowed with the burden of years and labors, he could write, "Beloved, think it not strange concerning the fiery trial which is to try you, as though some strange thing happened unto you: but rejoice, inasmuch as ye are partakers of Christ's sufferings; that, when His glory shall be revealed, ye may be glad also with exceeding joy." *Acts of the Apostles*, 525.

Peter's Martyrdom

The apostles Paul and Peter were for many years widely separated in their labors, it being the work of Paul to carry the gospel to the Gentiles, while Peter labored especially for the Jews. But in the providence of God, both were to bear witness for Christ in the world's metropolis, and upon its soil both were to shed their blood as the seed of a vast harvest of saints and martyrs.

About the time of Paul's second arrest, Peter also was apprehended and thrust into prison. He had made himself especially obnoxious to the authorities by his zeal and success in exposing the deceptions and defeating the plots of Simon Magus the sorcerer.

About the time of Paul's second arrest, Peter also was apprehended and thrust into prison. He had made himself especially obnoxious to the authorities by his zeal and success in exposing the deceptions and defeating the plots of Simon Magus the sorcerer, who had followed him to Rome to oppose and hinder the work of the gospel. Nero was a believer in magic, and had patronized

Simon. He was therefore greatly incensed against the apostle, and was thus prompted to order his arrest. …

Peter, as a Jew and a foreigner, was condemned to be scourged and crucified. In prospect of this fearful death, the apostle remembered his great sin in denying Jesus in the hour of trial, and his only thought was, that he was unworthy of so great an honor as to die in the same manner as did his Master. Peter had sincerely repented of that sin, and had been forgiven by Christ, as is shown by the high commission given him to feed the sheep and lambs of the flock. But he could never forgive himself. Not even the thought of the agonies of the last terrible scene could lessen the bitterness of his sorrow and repentance. As a last favor he entreated his executioners that he might be nailed to the cross with his head downward. The request was granted, and in this manner died the great apostle Peter. *Sketches from the Life of Paul*, 328, 329.

We invite you to view the complete
selection of titles we publish at:

www.TEACHServices.com

scan with your mobile
device to go directly
to our website

Please write or email us your praises, reactions, or
thoughts about this or any other book we publish at:

TEACH Services, Inc.

P U B L I S H I N G

www.TEACHServices.com ● (800) 367-1844

Info@TEACHServices.com

TEACH Services, Inc., titles may be purchased in bulk for
educational, business, fund-raising, or sales promotional use.
For information, please e-mail:

BulkSales@TEACHServices.com

Finally if you are interested in seeing
your own book in print, please contact us at

publishing@TEACHServices.com

We would be happy to review your manuscript for free.

www.ingramcontent.com/pod-product-compliance
Lightning Source LLC
Chambersburg PA
CBHW060552100426
42742CB00013B/2531